. BACK TO BASICS .

Traditional Garden Wisdom

"The man who has planted a garden feels that he has done something for the good of the world."

—VITA SACKVILLE-WEST

· BACK TO BASICS ·

Traditional Garden Wisdom

Time-Tested Techniques for Creating a Natural, Sustainable Outdoor Space

CHARLIE RYRIE AND ANNE HALPIN
CONTRIBUTING EDITORS

Reader's Digest

The Reader's Digest Association, Inc.
New York, New York | Montreal

A READER'S DIGEST BOOK

Copyright © 2011 Quintet Publishing Limited

All rights reserved. Unauthorized reproduction, in any manner, is prohibited.

Reader's Digest is a registered trademark of The Reader's Digest Association, Inc.

This book was designed and produced by Quintet Publishing Limited,
6 Blundell Street, London N7 9BH, UK

FOR QUINTET PUBLISHING
Project Editor Asha Savjani
Illustrator Bernard Chau
Additional Text Carly Beckerman-Boys
Designer Rod Teasdale
Art Director Michael Charles
Managing Editor Donna Gregory
Publisher James Tavendale

FOR READER'S DIGEST
U.S. Project Editor Kim Casey
Canadian Consulting Editors Jesse Corbeil, J. D. Gravenor
Project Designer Jennifer Tokarski
Senior Art Director George McKeon
Manager, English Book Editorial, Reader's Digest Canada Pamela Johnson
Executive Editor, Trade Publishing Dolores York
Associate Publisher, Trade Publishing Rosanne McManus
President and Publisher, Trade Publishing Harold Clarke

Library of Congress Cataloging-in-Publication Data

Back to basics : traditional garden wisdom : time-tested tips and techniques for creating a natural, sustainable outdoor space / Charlie Ryrie and Anne Halpin, contributing editors. -- 1st ed.
    p. cm.
  Traditional garden wisdom
  ISBN 978-1-60652-042-0
  1. Gardens--Design. 2. Gardening. I. Ryrie, Charlie. II. Halpin, Anne Moyer. III. Title: Traditional garden wisdom.
  SB473.B27 2011
  635--dc22
                                    2010030278

Note to Our Readers
The editors who produced this book have attempted to make the contents as accurate and correct as possible. Illustrations, photographs, and text have been carefully checked. All instructions should be reviewed and understood by the reader before undertaking any project.

We are committed to both the quality of our products and the service we provide to our customers. We value your comments, so please feel free to contact us.

The Reader's Digest Association, Inc.
Adult Trade Publishing
44 S. Broadway
White Plains, NY 10601

For more Reader's Digest products and information, visit our website:
    www.rd.com (in the United States)
    www.readersdigest.ca (in Canada)

QTT.BBG

Printed in China

10 9 8 7 6 5 4 3 2 1

CONTENTS

INTRODUCTION

Gardening used to be a part of life. Even people with humble homes in towns had small plots where they grew vegetables and a few flowers. Gardening skills used to be passed down from generation to generation, and until the middle of the twentieth century, it was normal for people to create their own gardens, often using materials they found around them and with plants they had propagated themselves or been given by friends. But in the last 60 years or so gardening has become big business. You can now easily buy just about any plant you want or garden materials from anywhere in the world. While it's wonderful to have such choices, at the same time many basic gardening skills have been handed over to plant breeders, plant sellers, and garden designers. People have lost the confidence to do it themselves.

BACK TO BASICS IN THE GARDEN

This book will give you the ability to enjoy gardening as naturally as possible without worrying about it. Anyone can garden, and the traditional ways are often the best. We're not suggesting that you go back to the primitive tools and techniques used thousands of years ago, but if we look back to our grandparents' generation and before, we can find some straightforward, time-tested, and thoroughly practical gardening methods. Many of these old-fashioned methods are environmentally sustainable, too. Combine them with modern innovations, such as packaged soil mixes and fertilizers for different purposes, ergonomically designed tools, automatic watering systems, and other advances, and you will find that gardening has never been easier.

Your Garden Is for You

For some people the backyard is all about enjoying outdoor space, just somewhere to spend time outside. There's nothing wrong with that, but you're probably not reading this book if all you want is a space to lounge or kick a ball. For most of us, gardens are also about plants and finding the best ways to make a space beautiful, and individual, with plants. The most successful gardens combine interesting structures with attractive planting, but beauty really is in the eye of the beholder. Something that one person finds beautiful may seem unappealing to someone else. It's the same with patios, paths, pergolas, and other structural elements. Some of us head toward a natural look with a fair degree of chaos around the edges, while others prefer a more formal or minimalist approach. It can't be stressed often enough that your garden is for you, suited to your taste, and for you to use the way you want. Don't worry for a moment about what other people might think; the best gardens are often the most personal. Do try to use the most natural, local materials you can. Why choose imported stone if you can find a local alternative? Don't buy plants when it's so much more satisfying to sow and grow your own, and do learn to garden with nature, using what it provides rather than fighting against it with artificial products and methods.

Much of gardening, even garden construction, is based on common sense. You won't find complicated construction projects in these pages, but you will find suggestions for ways to create the spaces you want with the skills you already have. When you know how things should be done, you can try anything if you want to. But if you decide a particular project is too daunting for you to tackle alone, there's no shame in calling in someone else to help. Learn the basics and you'll find that you can create your dream garden without spending a fortune. That's what this book aims to give you.

The main thing to remember is that gardening is not a stressful, competitive activity; it's fun. Your garden is for you, your family, and friends, and the best gardens always reflect that. Don't ever worry about getting everything perfect, about whether your garden is as good as someone else's. Each garden is unique. The only rule is that gardening should be enjoyable. If it isn't, you probably shouldn't be doing it.

BEFORE YOU START

To get really good results and a garden you can be proud of, the first step is careful planning. There's no point in planting violets if your garden gets full sun, and some plants, such as sunflowers and roses, might require more time than you have to spare. Planning ensures that your burgeoning garden never becomes victim to common beginner pitfalls. Magazines and helpful sales clerks will also recommend a whole host of tools and equipment you don't actually need, or at least won't need for a while, so planning your garden in advance saves time, money, and hassle while you learn the ropes.

What do you want in your garden? Flowers? Homegrown produce? A relaxing space, or play area for the children? Taking these considerations into account, you can create the ideal outdoor space for your needs, getting the most out of its position and climate. For example, St. Augustine grass might be hard and spiky, but sandy soil turns most other varieties brown. If you plan correctly from the start, you can sidestep such confusing issues as your beautiful new garden bears the fruits of your labor.

ASSESSING YOUR SPACE

Before you make any decisions about your garden, take a really good look at what you're starting with. Look around the space from ground level, from different angles, then go upstairs and see what it looks like from the upstairs windows. Take notes of what you see, and take photos, too; you may see things slightly differently through a photograph. Walk around the garden and make a note of sunny and shady areas, see if you need shelter, for plants or for people. Find out whether some areas are very dry, or particularly damp. Check whether wind is a problem, and see where you're most exposed.

Think about what you want from a garden. Make a wish list of everything you would like to have, perhaps under the headings of recreation, planting, structures, and utility. You may want spaces for relaxing, sunbathing, entertaining, and a children's play area. Do you want to grow vegetables? Do you dream of flowing perennial borders or billows of climbing roses? Do you want a patio, a lawn, or a pond? Is there room for a shed?

Add to the list everything you will definitely need on a practical level, too. This may include screening, windbreaks, steps or terraces on a slope, removing large plants to let in more sun, paths, tool storage, and a clothesline. Safety is an important consideration, especially for children and elderly people.

No man but feels more of a man in the world if he can have a bit of ground that he can call his own. However small it is on the surface, it is four thousand miles deep; and that is a very handsome property.

—Charles Dudley Warner

START SMALL

If you are new to gardening, the best advice is to start small. It is easy to overestimate how much time you will be able to spend on your garden. You can always expand the garden next year.

TAKE A SECOND LOOK

When you have a good idea of what you want, and what you need, take another look at the existing garden. Can you fit in everything on your wish list? How much time do you have to look after it all? Be realistic. Then reassess your list, ranking items in order of importance, and see if anything can go. For example, on a small property is it crucial to have a lawn or would paving or gravel be more sensible? Do you need a barbecue if the garden opens straight from the kitchen? Is there really space for a patio or rambling roses?

Ask Yourself

The two most important questions are: How will you use your garden? How much time do you want to spend looking after it?

Structures Arches, arbors, water feature, cold frame

Utility Garden storage, clothesline

Recreation Patio, sitting space, play area

Plants Trees, shrubs, hedges, perennial and annual flowers, roses, vegetables, containers

Making Your Own Rustic Arbor

A rustic arbor is a fun way of supporting climbing plants and dividing spaces in your garden. Making one is not really about following plans; it's about what you can find and your design inspiration. But there are some tips to follow whatever design you create.

Here's how to make a simple arbor 7 feet (2.1 m) tall by 6 feet (1.8 m) wide by 6 feet (1.8 m) long to frame a path or gateway.

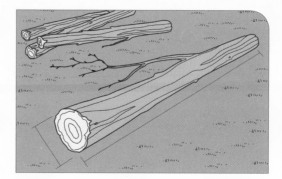

1 Choose the right materials. It's fine to use whatever fallen and felled branches and brush you can find in your own yard and neighborhood, but remember that your structure will last only as long as the wood you use. Red cedar is particularly popular because it lasts well and is resistant to both rot and termites. You need about 12 logs, each 4–5 inches (10–13 cm) in diameter, at least 8 feet (2.4 m) long for the posts and any main cross beams, and a selection of smaller diameter lumber (which you can buy from a lumberyard or obtain from your garden by cutting small branches from trees) to fill spaces in between. You can place your arbor on paving slabs, but if you want to sink your structure into the ground (which will make it sturdier) allow 12–18 inches (30–46 cm) of extra length for each main post.

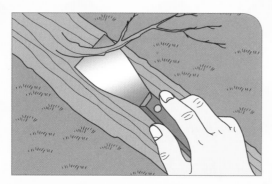

2 Leaving the bark intact looks more rustic, but it can mean that bugs and moisture will congregate and rot will set in early. It's a good idea to strip the bark by scraping it off the posts with a chisel or paint scraper. Treat the ends of each log by painting them with wood preservative to help preserve them. Do the same wherever you drill holes.

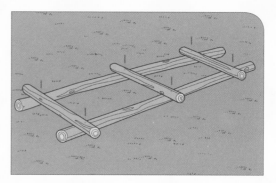

3 Lay out the logs to make the sides of your arbor as near as possible to where you want to place your structure. A simple ladder shape is effective. It looks best if you let the ends of each horizontal post stick out 1–2 inches (2.5–5 cm) beyond the verticals, and the verticals should poke out 1–2 inches (2.5–5 cm) above the topmost vertical posts. Drill holes through the pairs of logs to fasten the posts and cross timbers together using galvanized screws or carriage bolts. Make each side on the ground, and affix the top section later.

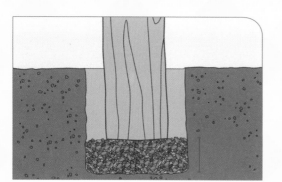

4 Plant the main supporting poles of your side structure into holes with around 4 inches (10 cm) of gravel at the base, then fill with concrete. Leave it to harden for at least 24 hours, then attach your top crosspieces.

WORKING WITH WHAT YOU HAVE

You can change most things in a garden, but you can't alter the way your garden faces, and the amount of sun it gets. The first thing to do is to work out how the sun moves across your garden, to discover which areas are in sun or shade at certain times of the day. Look out of your windows and walk around your garden at different times of day, and in different seasons, too, to see which parts are in shade or sun at different times. Make some diagrams or notes so you remember.

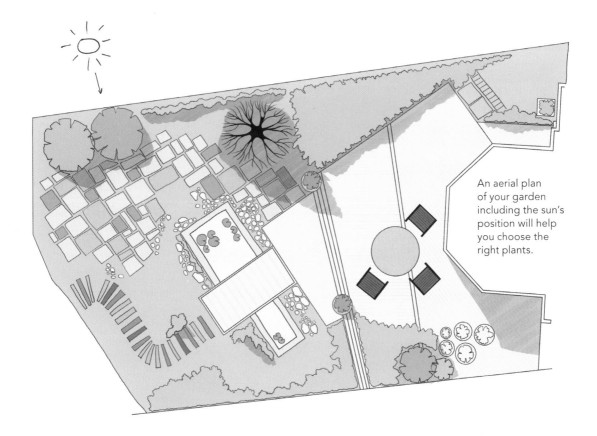

An aerial plan of your garden including the sun's position will help you choose the right plants.

If a large tree or shrub throws out a huge amount of shade, you may be able to take it down or cut it back, but you can't change the way the walls of buildings or neighbor's boundaries may shade your garden. You don't want to cut down any large, old trees unless absolutely necessary—we need our trees to produce oxygen and store carbon dioxide.

Think about which existing features you need to keep, and which you want to take out. It is often tempting to remove everything and start with a fresh canvas. But don't be in too much of a hurry to bulldoze your existing landscape. There's nothing like a few well-established trees or clumps of smaller plants to give maturity to a new garden, and features such as well-established hedges are very hard to replace.

KEEP THE PATIO

If there is an existing patio, can you work with its shape or adapt it? A patio is expensive to remove and replace, so at least try to keep the base even if you change the surface materials.

20 Great Plants for Shade

Aquilegia spp., columbine	*Geranium* spp., cranesbill
Aruncus dioicus, goatsbeard	*Hakonechloa macra* 'Aureola', Hakone grass
Astilbe spp.	*Helleborus* spp., hellebores
Aucuba japonica, gold dust plant	*Heuchera* spp., alumroot
Begonia spp.	*Hosta* spp.
Caladium x *hortulanum*	*Hydrangea petiolaris*, climbing hydrangea
Chrysogonum virginianum, green-and-gold	*Ilex crenata*, Japanese holly
Epimedium spp., bishop's hat	*Kerria japonica*, Japanese kerria
Ferns	*Rhododendron* spp., azalea and rhododendron
Gaultheria shallon, salal	*Tiarella cordifolia*, foamflower

20 Great Plants for Dry Soil

Argyranthemum spp., Marguerite daisy	*Lantana* cvs.
Baptisia australis, blue false indigo	*Liatris* spp., gayfeather
Callistemon spp., bottlebrush	*Mahonia* spp., Oregon grape
Catharanthus roseus, Madagascar periwinkle	*Myrica pensylvanica, M. cerifera*, bayberry, wax myrtle
Ceanothus spp., California lilac	*Nepeta* x *faassenii*, catmint
Cercidium floridum, palo verde	*Phormium tenax*, New Zealand flax
Echinacea purpurea, purple coneflower	*Portulacca grandiflora*, rose moss
Gaillardia grandiflora, blanketflower	*Rhus* spp., sumac
Iris germanica, bearded iris	*Rudbeckia* spp., black-eyed Susan
Juniperus spp., junipers	*Zauschneria californica*, California fuchsia

20 Great Plants for Wet Places

Acer rubrum, red maple	*Halesia carolina*, Carolina silverbell
Aster novae-angliae, New England aster	*Hibiscus moscheutos*, rose mallow
Astilbe spp.	*Iris ensata*, Japanese iris
Betula nigra 'Heritage', river birch	*Lindera benzoin*, spicebush
Caltha palustris, marsh marigold	*Lobelia cardinalis*, cardinal flower
Cimicifuga racemosa, black snakeroot	*Nyssa sylvatica*, tupelo
Clethra alnifolia, sweet pepperbush	*Rodgersia* spp.
Cornus stolonifera, red-osier dogwood	*Salix babyonica*, weeping willow
Eupatorium purpureum, Joe-pye weed	*Thalictrum* spp., meadow rue
Filipendula spp., meadowsweet	*Zantedeschia aethiopica*, calla lily

Recycling Existing Features

While you might want to start afresh with a totally new space, it's creative and cost-effective to incorporate recycled features into your overall garden design.

Circles of trunk from a recently removed tree can be used as stepping stones.

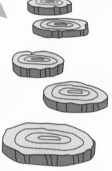

Timber from an old shed or fence can be used to build compost bins. Make sure one side is removable to allow access.

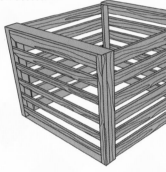

Old storm windows can have a new life as cold frames.

Before you get out the spade and the chainsaw, think about whether some plants could be moved, pruned, or saved. Could an old shed be revamped or given a new use?

Another good reason to go slow at this stage is because what's in your landscape now probably holds good clues for how to use your garden. There may be a very good reason why a shed is placed where it is, why there is a tall boundary fence, or why a pathway is positioned in a particular place. Also plants that are already in place can give you a good idea of what will grow happily in your garden. Study the plants on your property to see which ones are thriving and which are struggling, and try to figure out why. They may be getting too much or too little sunlight or water, there may be soil problems, or deer may be eating them. Understanding what's problematic now will help you avoid making the same mistakes again.

It is also important to assess the growing conditions available to plants in different parts of your yard. Then you can select plants likely to thrive there.

Don't cut down a healthy, large tree unless it is absolutely necessary. But if you really cannot live with something, such as a large tree, get a professional in to remove it. Apart from the mammoth task of cutting up and disposing of an entire tree, old trees have large root systems and when they are removed very serious subsidence can occur. It's not a job worth tackling yourself. Removing an evergreen hedge is always a job for a professional, because the trees or shrubs will have substantial roots.

WAYS TO LET MORE LIGHT INTO A SHADY GARDEN

If the shade comes from dense foliage, it may help to remove some limbs from trees or cut back rampant climbers and tall hedges. If buildings block the light you can brighten the space with paint and mirrors. A white or pale-colored wall or fence will attract any available light, a small pool can reflect light from above, and a carefully placed mirror will bounce reflected rays into your space.

Which Way Does Your Garden Grow?

The direction your garden faces can affect the types of plants that will thrive in it.

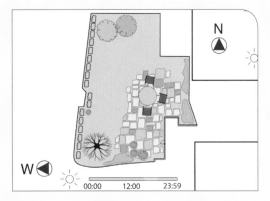

West-facing Gets afternoon and early evening sun. In a northern climate, a garden facing west can be ideal for sitting areas and most sun-loving plants. In southern areas it would be uncomfortably hot in summer without shade.

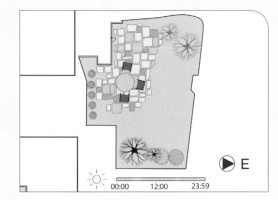

East-facing Gets morning sun and afternoon shade. Sun-loving plants will survive as long as they're not too shaded. Perfect for a morning sitting area.

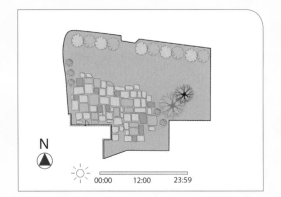

North-facing The coldest, dimmest area, gets little direct light if overhung with trees or hedge. Best suits shade lovers.

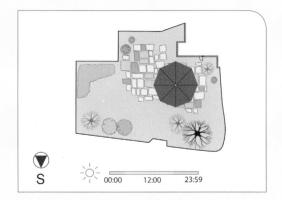

South-facing Sunny most of the day, from morning to late afternoon. This area can bake in summer. Ideal for Mediterranean, heat-loving and slightly tender plants and for vegetables and herbs that need full sun. A patio will need shade.

COMBINE DESIGN WITH COMMON SENSE

Good old-fashioned common sense is the best design tool of all. You know what you want from the space, so you are the best person for the job. If you don't know much about plants, you can get help from friends, books, and nurseries. However, only you know what you really want from your outdoor space.

Here are some things to consider when designing your garden. How will you actually use it? Be honest here. You may dream of lounging on designer furniture with a cocktail in your hand, but is the reality more likely to be flopping onto a comfy chair at the end of a busy day to take in the view and wondering how anyone ever has time to garden?

What is your house like? If it is minimalist and uncluttered, you'll probably be happiest with a formal or unfussy garden, but if your house has a touch of chaos around the edges, you'll probably want an informal relaxed garden, too. You may dream of clipped edges and ordered spaces. But if you're just not the type of person to work at it all the time, you'll find it far from relaxing. If you're undecided, you can have the best of both worlds and have a small formal area within a wilder garden or vice versa.

Be realistic about how much time you have to spend. If your life is already busy you probably don't want the pressure of a demanding garden to boot. Low maintenance doesn't have to be all hard surfaces and lawn chairs; you can opt for a touch of wilderness or choose low-maintenance planting schemes that can be every bit as effective as time-consuming flower borders. For example, you could plant shrubs with flowers or colored foliage, or easy-care ornamental grasses instead of perennials and annuals. If you do want a flower garden, seek out flowers that don't require a lot of deadheading and fussing.

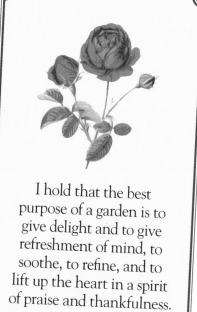

I hold that the best purpose of a garden is to give delight and to give refreshment of mind, to soothe, to refine, and to lift up the heart in a spirit of praise and thankfulness.

—Gertrude Jekyll

20 Great Low-Maintenance Perennials

Artemisia spp.	*Iris sibirica*, Siberian iris
Asclepias tuberosa, butterfly weed	*Liatris* spp., gayfeather
Brunnera macrophylla, Siberian bugloss	*Liriope spicata*, lilyturf
Ceratostigma plumbaginoides, plumbago	*Perovskia atriplicifolia*, Russian sage
Chelone lyonii, turtlehead	*Physostegia virginiana*, obedient plant
Coreopsis verticillata, threadleaf coreopsis	*Platycodon grandiflorus*, balloon flower
Echinops ritro, globe thistle	*Pulmonaria* spp., lungwort
Geranium spp., cranesbill	*Salvia nemorosa*
Helianthemum nummularium, rock rose	*Tiarella cordifolia*, foamflower
Heuchera spp., alumroot	*Tricyrtis hirta*, toad lily

SEASONAL GARDENING TASKS

Regardless of climate, your garden goes through seasonal changes throughout the year. Some places have less defined seasons, but scheduling garden tasks annually helps to ensure optimum results.

Main Spring Tasks

Spring is the busiest time for gardening, so get started early to avoid unnecessary weeding.

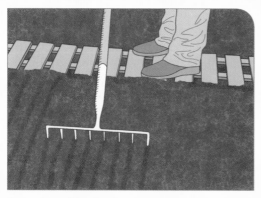

Preparing soil for planting

Preparing vegetable beds

Sowing seeds and looking after seedlings

Planting annuals and new perennials

Mowing, (weeding, and feeding) the lawn

Feeding flower beds

Main Summer Tasks

Summer is the time to enjoy the fruits of your labor. Perennials, bedding plants, and rose bushes need plenty of weeding and watering to keep them looking healthy for the entire season.

Main Fall/Winter Tasks

Fall and winter gardening involves maintenance and preparation. While tidying your garden for any upcoming inclement weather, you also need to fertilize for the next growing season.

Thinning seedlings

Raking leaves

Weeding beds

Clipping hedges

Watering plants

Fertilizing lawn with slow-release nitrogen

DESIGN TRICKS

Getting proportions right in your garden is important. It's like positioning furniture in a room, trying to get a balance between the different elements. Instead of working with furniture and floor space, you need to achieve a balance between plants and garden features, and the spaces between them, such as lawns, patios, and paths. Aim to make the shapes on the ground in proportion to the house and site. However, you can also play with scale. A dramatic large plant can make a small space appear much larger, though a huge solid structure in a small space will dwarf it. Just as a small room full of knickknacks will seem extremely cluttered, lots of small plants will emphasize the limited size of a small garden.

Plant houseleeks (*Sempervivum*) in the crevices of walls to protect the garden and keep out lightning.

Defining Garden Spaces

The way you enter your garden and move through it is important.

Make the most of your entrance (you'll use it constantly), and make your paths interesting as well as functional. Paths are necessary for you to move through the landscape, so decide how you want to move through your space. You will need fairly direct routes from your gate or where you park the car to the door of your house to get to garden utility areas, a shed, compost bins, clotheslines, and trash cans. These paths don't have to be straight lines, but don't make them pointlessly complicated, or you may end up skipping over the grass or jumping over flowers rather than following the path.

Paths are also design elements, so you need to consider that, too. A long, straight path suggests rapid movement and appears more formal, while a curving path that disappears behind plants or a structure gives a more relaxed pace and appears more informal. A garden that can't be seen all at once is more interesting than a space where everything is immediately obvious. Even in a square, flat garden you can add vertical structures, such as solid or living fences, panels of trellis, arches, and pergolas. Next you can provide small openings to give enticing glimpses of what is beyond. Use plants as well as structures and landscaping to bring movement into your garden. A patch of tall bamboos, for example, can act as an effective screen and will also provide movement and sound as their leaves rustle in the slightest breeze. Ornamental grasses and many tall, slender perennials, such as black-eyed Susans (*Rudbeckia nitida* 'Herbstonne'), Siberian iris (*Iris sibirica*), burnet or bottlebrush (*Sanguisorba* spp.), meadowsweet (*Thalictrum* spp.), and *Verbena bonariensis* will also whisper and move at a touch of wind.

Making the Most of Your Space

Creating the ideal garden is about finding what works for you. An enormous backyard has endless design possibilities, but areas often considered pokey or awkward can make equally stunning gardens with a little space-enhancing advice.

Narrow gardens can be made to look wider by setting the layout on the diagonal—the lines move the eye around the garden rather than fixing on boundaries.

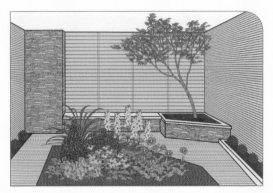

Create a sense of depth in a shallow garden by bringing generous areas of planting into the center of the space.

20 Great Climbers for Arches, Arbors, and Pergolas

Actinidia kolomikta, kolomikta vine	*Laburnum* x *watereri*, golden chain tree
Akebia quinata, five-leaf akebia	*Parthenocissus tricuspidata*, Boston ivy
Aristolochia californica, *A. durior*, Dutchman's pipe	*Passiflora* spp., passionflower
Bougainvillea cvs. (warm climates)	*Polygonum aubertii*, silverlace vine
Campsis radicans, trumpet creeper	*Rosa* cvs., climbing roses
Clematis spp. and cvs.	*Solanum jasminoides*, potato vine (warm climates)
Gelsemium sempervirens, Carolina jessamine (warm climates)	*Tecomaria capensis*, Cape honeysuckle
	Trachelospermum jasminoides, Confederate jasmine
Humulus spp., hops	*Vitis* spp., grapes
Ipomoea spp., morning glories (annual)	*Wisteria* spp. (but be aware that this needs a very sturdy structure)
Jasminum spp., jasmines	

Clematis is a great climber for arches, arbors, and pergolas.

WORK WITH SHAPES

Angular and diagonal shapes encourage movement through a space. Circles and squares are static, making pleasing lawns, pools, or meandering paths.

Framing or Hiding the View

In urban areas surrounding roofs and rooflines can be beautiful, particularly if they include fine old trees or perhaps church towers. Country gardens may have lovely views outside the boundaries. Try and frame interesting views with well-placed trees, shrubs, and structures. But if the view beyond your garden is nothing special, aim to keep attention within the garden with strong focal points, such as striking specimen plants, ornaments, or art and interesting features. Provide an eye-catching feature, plant, or structure at the far end of the garden or at any point you want to emphasize, and let the planting lead your eye there.

Making a Small Garden Feel Bigger

Focal Points
Whether it's a small manicured lawn or flower bed, a central focal point will make a garden with limited space feel larger.

Soften the edges of a square or rectangular garden with curves, which will also create a feeling of increased space. But you don't have to steer clear of straight lines in informal gardens. Soften the edges of a simple straight path with plants, or use paving materials with interesting shapes and textures, such as cobbles or irregular tiles.

COMBINE DIFFERENT PLANT SHAPES

Shapes are important for every element of your garden. Choose plants for their shape and foliage texture as well as for the color of their flowers. A mix of different shapes—bushy, spiky, feathery, bold—makes for a more interesting garden.

Plants to Soften Garden Edges

Abronia villosa, sand verbena	*Impatiens* cvs., bedding impatiens
Arabis spp., rock cress	*Lampranthus* spp., ice plant
Armeria juniperifolia, thrift	*Lobularia maritima*, sweet alyssum
Artemisia schmidtiana 'Nana', silver mound	*Nierembergia caerulea*, cup flower
Begonia semperflorens, wax begonia	*Petunia* cvs., wave petunia
Ceratostigma plumbaginoides, leadwort	*Sanvitalia procumbens*, creeping zinnia
Dianthus gratianopolitanus, cheddar pink	*Stachys byzantina*, lamb's ears
Geranium sanguineum var. striatum, Lancaster geranium	*Tagetes* spp., French marigold, signet marigold
Gomphrena globosa, globe amaranth	*Tropaeolum majus*, nasturtium
Iberis sempervirens, perennial candytuft	*Zinnia haageana*, narrow-leaved zinnia

Another trick to give a feeling of increased space is to change levels and create distinct spaces. The best solution for a steep slope is to make terraced raised beds to create space and interest with different layers of planting—and it offers the opportunity for interesting steps. But if your slope is slight and you have young children, leave it for now. Children love playing on gentle slopes, and steps can be problematic for youngsters. Internal divisions in the garden do not need to be tall. Low, clipped hedges of boxwood or herbs, such as lavender or rosemary, are wonderful for marking out different areas within a garden. Being able to look out over different areas brings a feeling of depth to a garden.

WORKING WITH COLOR

If you're planning a flower garden, be sure to think about color. A predominantly pastel-colored garden feels much calmer and softer than a vibrant garden full of hot reds and oranges, while cool whites and blues with paler greens create a very tranquil space. For contemplative areas steer toward mauves, pale blues, creams, and soft pinks with greens (though many gardeners like to spice up a pastel garden with a few sparks of hot reds and yellows for pleasing contrast). A few carefully placed spots of a bright color will intensify rather than clash with calmer colors. Don't forget to consider the colors of foliage, from all the myriad greens through plants with white, silver, yellow-edged, or splashed leaves. There are also red, yellow, and purple foliages. A mass of silver-leaved plants can enhance a very sunny space, while acid greens and white-splashed or variegated leaves are well suited to shadier gardens.

Don't be afraid of color. Painted fences and furniture can transform an ordinary space into something striking. Blue and green tones work best in cooler northern hemisphere gardens, brighter hues look good where there is more sun. Choose colors for garden structures that work with the color scheme of the garden and with the exterior colors of your home. The color of a gate can echo the trim on your house, for example, and harmonize or contrast pleasingly with the flowers in the garden.

Drama in the Garden
The smallest spaces can be made larger and grander with theatrical touches, such as a door going nowhere set into a wall, strategically placed mirrors, or carefully sited lighting.

COLOR TRICKS

In the garden warm colors come forward visually and cool colors recede. To make a large, sprawling garden seem more intimate, use lots of warm, bright colors. To make a small garden look bigger, use cool, pale colors.

PUTTING IDEAS ON PAPER

When you have a good idea of what you want to include in your garden, put your ideas on paper. It's not as daunting as it sounds. Some people make beautiful detailed plans, and some of us make rougher working drawings. The point is to come up with one coherent design rather than lots of little bits and pieces at random. If you like drawing, start from a photograph of your garden blown up to 8½ x 11 size on a photocopier or computer printer, if you are using a digital camera. Put some tracing paper over the enlarged photo and mark the elements you're keeping, then sketch in your new ideas. Take your time and use as many sheets of tracing paper as you need until you get an idea of what goes where.

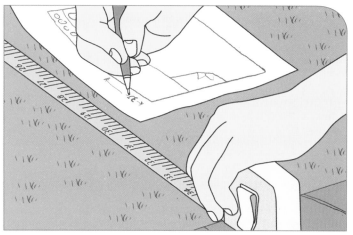

Drawing to Scale
Though it's possible to draw a plan of your garden on plain paper, some people find graph paper is useful for accuracy and double-checking measurements and straight lines.

Making a Plan to Scale

The next step is to make a scale plan, an overhead view of your garden reduced to a convenient size to fit onto a piece of paper. For this you need to measure your existing garden accurately. You need a good measuring tape, preferably a second pair of hands for extra help, and a pencil and paper to jot down the measurements.

To measure up, walk around the garden and put physical marks at approximately 3-foot (1-m) intervals around the perimeter. Mark and measure the position of windows and doors—they will influence where you put patios, paths, and focal points—then transfer your measurements onto a sheet of graph paper. Your scale will depend on the size of your garden—the larger the garden, the smaller the scale needed to show it on one piece of paper. You'll find 1:100 is a useful scale, with one square representing one square foot (0.3 sq m), but use your common sense, too. The plan needs to be large enough to be useful but small enough to be manageable. Mark the scale at the bottom of your piece of paper. Check the aspect (the compass direction) of your garden and indicate this on your plan.

Next plot the positions and dimensions of anything you want to keep, such as mature trees, key plants, sheds, patios, and ponds. Measure the distance to each feature from fixed points, such as one edge of the house, a boundary fence, or the wall of a shed. Measure the girth and canopy of large trees as the shady areas they create will affect planting and where you place features, such as sitting areas or ponds. You also should mark things you will have to remove.

Then stick tracing paper overlays over the main sheet and mark your planned new features and design ideas on them. Do this in pencil, or keep lots of sheets of tracing paper handy so you can adjust your plan several times as you realize that certain

PLAN ON A SURVEY

If you have a copy of your property survey, you can enlarge it instead of using a photo as the basis for your landscape plan. The survey will have existing driveways and other features already marked on it.

features are going to be too close, too formal, too unrelated, or plain unnecessary.

Reexamine Your Design

When you've put all the elements of your design onto paper, it is time to reconsider. The most common mistake is to pack too many things into one space, so make sure that items aren't too close together, and that one feature doesn't interfere with another. Have you left enough space for plants to grow outward as well as upward? Do the routes around and through the garden look balanced? Do you have enough or too much symmetry?

Double-check the drawing against the compass points. It's easy to forget about the shade cast by a neighbor's tree or building. Check that you are putting beds in the best places, that a pond will not be overhung by deciduous trees, that an arbor will get enough sun, and a patio will get some shade. Make sure you are choosing the best places for sun-loving or shade-loving plants as well as sun-loving and shade-loving people!

Remember that plants grow outward as well as up. A tree can overshadow a sunny bed in as little as five years. Be sure to allow enough space for trees and shrubs to reach their mature size.

Finishing Your Blueprint

Check against the compass positions to make sure you are planning beds and seating in the right spots. For example, a west-facing spot is lovely for a sitting area to catch afternoon sun if you live in the North. A vegetable garden ideally wants maximum eastern exposure if you live in the South. Sun-loving plants want a clear southern exposure if you live in the North. Make a note on your drawing of different conditions—shady, windy, dry soil, problems with surface roots or drainage pipes.

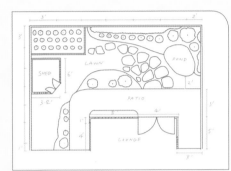

Planning in Advance
Creating a blueprint ensures that your garden reflects your personality, lifestyle, and needs.

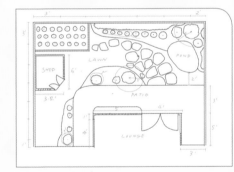

Making Alterations
Trying out new ideas and then making alterations at the planning stage will ensure your budget (large or small) is spent wisely.

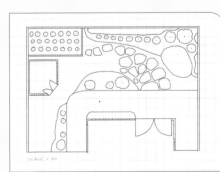

Scale Drawing
Although it's time consuming, always do a scale drawing. This allows you to plan with accuracy and avoid costly surprises when planting or building.

LAYING OUT THE GARDEN

When you're happy with your design on paper, transfer it to the ground. For a really accurate job you need clothespins or metal stakes, a tape measure, and a string line of fine nylon or cotton string. Once you've marked out all your features, copy the lines onto the ground with landscape marking paint.

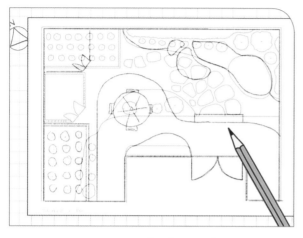

Mark straight lines by fixing string to pegs or small stakes at no more than 12-foot (4-m) intervals along the length, closer together in a small plot. Insert the two end pegs first and stretch a line between them, then insert intermediate pegs just touching the line. Then undo the line and fix it to each peg with a double loop.

Circles are easily marked. Place a stake at the center point, then attach a piece of rope or string and mark the radius length on it. Keep this taut and walk around the central stake, spraying the circle on the ground as you go.

Once your plan is marked on the ground, double-check it. Have you forgotten anything? Can you get a wheelbarrow from A to B? Have you left space for storage—do you need to? Is every path wide enough? Are your beds in sun/shade? Will you get sun/shade on a sitting area when you want it? Is there really room for that barbecue/sitting area/children's jungle gym?

Go back to the drawing board and make minor alterations on your plan and the ground as many times as you need. Getting it right at this stage saves infinite hassle later.

Get It Right
If you've laid out your plan on the garden and something isn't quite right, don't just leave it. There's no point putting in the hard work for a beautiful garden if the original design is flawed. Make the change; the extra effort is always worth it.

Making the Most of Your Space

Creating the ideal garden is about finding what works for you. An enormous backyard has endless design possibilities, but areas often considered pokey or awkward can make equally stunning gardens with a little space-enhancing advice.

Simple materials, such as string, a tape measure, and wooden or metal pegs are all you need to mark up a garden design.

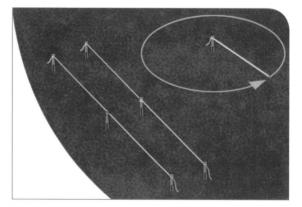

Landscape marking paint is also useful for laying out some straight lines and circular or irregular shapes.

Making Right Angles—the 3:4:5 Principle

Square or rectangular beds and paving need accurate right angles. To lay these out you use probably the only piece of geometry you'll ever need to know—the Pythagorean theorem. This states that any triangle that has side lengths in the ratio of 3:4:5 must be a right triangle, so as long as a 3:4:5 ratio is maintained, any triangle will have a right angle.

Suppose you want a rectangular bed with sides measuring 9 x 12 feet (3 x 4 m) or with side lengths in the ratio 3:4. Align the 12-foot (4-m) edge AB to a fixed point, such as a wall or fence and mark it accurately with stakes and string.

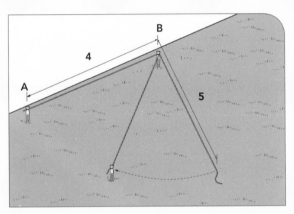

1 Take another longer piece of line, or your tape measure, fix it firmly to end B of the 12-foot (4-m) line and mark an end point 15 feet (5 m) along it. This is the third part of the 3:4:5 ratio.

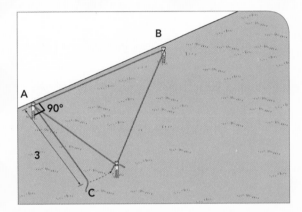

2 Holding the string or tape, walk diagonally toward where you think the shorter 9-foot (3-m) line BC should end, and pin the string into the ground at the 15-foot (5-m) point.

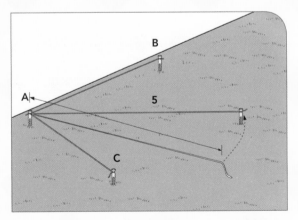

3 Take another piece of line or tape measure, attach it to the point A of the 12-foot (4-m) edge, mark it at 9 feet (3 m). Where the 9-foot (3-m) and 15-foot (5-m) lines cross at point C means BC is a straight line at a right angle to AB.

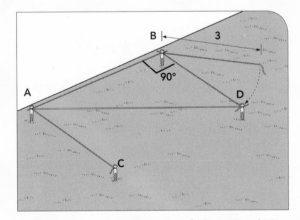

4 Repeat the process to find point D for lines AD and BD. Once you get the hang of this, you'll be able to work out right angles for beds or features of any dimensions.

DRAWING UP A WORK PLAN

Before you throw yourself into the activity of making your dream garden, you need to think about a schedule for getting the work done. Planning the order of the jobs means the project will be a pleasure rather than a nightmare.

A garden with a more natural approach, perhaps making recycled structures and using found materials, involves less planning at this stage. But at the very least you need to make sure you can get rid of anything you're removing and organize space to bring in new materials.

Digging Out Foundations

For any new building projects, such as sheds, walls, or greenhouses, you'll need to dig foundations. The size and shape will depend on the structure you are erecting, but the foundations should always be wider than the building project itself.

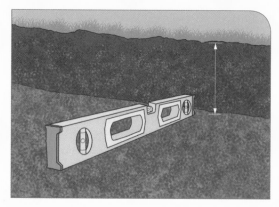

1 Clear the ground and remove any plant material or debris.

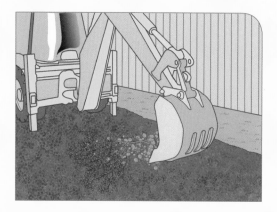

2 Dig down 6 inches (15 cm). Make sure the ground is level; check with a spirit level.

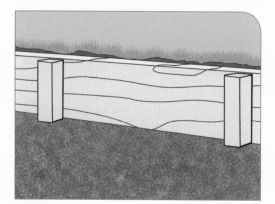

3 Put shuttering boards around any foundations that meet grass or earth.

4 Lay 2 inches (5 cm) of fill, topping with a layer of concrete, and level with the back of a rake.

Steps to Organize Your Space

1. Find out where you can dump stuff you're taking out of your space.

2. Take out any trees or shrubs you are removing.

3. Demolish old paths, patios, and old structures that can't get a new lease on life. Break up concrete structures with a sledgehammer to use as fill hardcore for new foundations, if needed.

4. If machinery is coming into your garden or you're doing serious construction, protect any vulnerable trees and shrubs with boards or any temporary barriers, and tie up vulnerable branches.

5. Dig out the foundations for any new hard structures—sheds, walls, greenhouses, patios, ponds, and paths.

6. Make trenches for water pipes and lay ducting for electricity.

7. Lay any concrete and hardcore.

8. Cut out new beds and clear the surface area of all areas where you'll be planting. If you're creating a new lawn, clear and cultivate the area before sowing or laying sod. Dig well-rotted compost into all planting areas.

9. Erect trellis, fencing, sheds, and any timber structures.

10. Organize delivery of paving materials, sand, and cement. Hire a builder to move manhole covers, if necessary.

11. Lay hard surfaces and install lighting, if desired.

12. Plant your new beds.

13. Lay or sow lawn.

Plan your garden layout when the moon is waxing. According to ancient tradition, we are all wiser under a waxing moon, and that's the time to do any work requiring thought.

KEEP PLANTS IN SCALE

To figure out the best size for the tallest plants in a garden bed, measure the width of the bed. The heights of the tallest plants when they mature should be about half the width of the bed.

THE BASIC ELEMENTS

Before you start to dig, it's important to think about the key elements you want in your garden. You can have a space free from almost all structures, except perhaps the occasional fence and a gate, so it relies only on the natural shape of the ground and any beds of plants you want to incorporate. Or you can add to the atmosphere of your yard with arches or arbors, interesting edgings, or a decorative water feature.

If you go the natural route, you can make a formal boundary with an evergreen hedge or create an informal screen with a mix of evergreen hollies or rhododendrons with deciduous native plants. If you choose to use man-made materials or structures to influence the feel of your garden, you can establish an outdoor living room with a patio or a deck; there is a wide spectrum of materials to choose from, including stone slabs, modern brick, cobblestones, or Belgian block. The choice is yours.

Making initial decisions on the basic elements of your yard will provide you with a solid base on which to build. Whether you're creating the garden of your dreams or making the best of an awkward space, this is the place where it all begins.

STRUCTURAL ELEMENTS OF THE LANDSCAPE

There's such a vast range of materials available for use in landscaping, including recycled materials. A fence made from driftwood or odd-sized remnants of lumber can be just as interesting as an expensive version of handmade metal or beautifully crafted traditional hardwood. A rustic arbor from branches and twigs cut from the backyard can be as beautiful as an intricate wrought-iron gazebo. You can make wonderful structures, from the practical to the fanciful, from bent and woven branches and twigs of willow, mulberry, or birch trees.

PAVING MATERIALS

The materials you use impact your garden as much as the plants you choose. If you're using new materials, it's best to keep to a minimal palette for the bulk of your landscaping. For example, if you're using mainly stone and wrought iron, don't add new red brick or concrete to the mix. Also make sure your materials complement your house; if your house is made of brick, a brick wall or brick paths would work well. For a wood-frame house, wood fences are a good match. However, you can use any number of natural materials together.

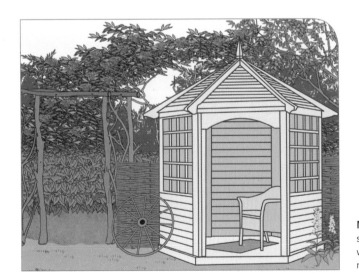

Matching If you have wooden structures in your garden, a wooden fence is often a better match than a stone wall.

For example, stone, brick, gravel, and tiles will blend effortlessly in a path, and many recycled materials are so perfect for your landscape it would be a crime not to use them. Some good examples of recycled materials are crushed seashells—a by-product of the shellfish industry and natural snail repellent—granulated CDs, and recycled glass chips to use in place of gravel, dress containers, or create paths and mulches.

A Variety of Step Styles

No matter which style of step you select for your garden, they will be subject to weather conditions. Steps will get slippery in the rain, so allow for longer treads than indoor steps and for room to drain.

Gravel held in place with wooden risers is inexpensive and effective.

Cobbles and tiles set behind a wooden riser look beautiful in a country garden.

Brick steps are most suitable for a brick house—try to match materials where possible.

Paving stones laid on top of a stone-wall riser are suitable for any garden style. Edge them with stone in formal gardens.

GATES AND ENTRANCES

There are as many ways to enter a garden as there are types of gardener. If you have a fairly formal garden, you may want an elegant metal or hardwood gate set in a hedge or wall, hung from stone or brick pillars topped with balls or obelisks, and perhaps surmounted by an ornate arch. It could be a single gate or a pair, and the gate could be solid, hiding what's inside, or more open to give a glimpse of the garden. An informal entrance could be a simple low wood or metal gate in a fence or hedge, or a door attached to a post set into a hedge or wall. An arch or arbor framed with climbing roses, honeysuckle, morning glories, or other flowering vines makes a lovely, inviting entry. Or you can train and trim a hedge to have an arch in it, for a living entry.

The width as well as the style of a gate depends on how you need to use the garden. If you have only one way to get inside, you need to make sure the entrance allows for generous access. However, if you only need space to walk through, you can be more inventive. Gates come in many styles. They may be sleek wood panels, rustic branches or poles, scrolled and filigreed, or plain wrought iron—the possibilities are endless. A low, slatted wooden or picket gate suits an informal entrance. Something more solid or substantial is fitting for a more formal entrance, and a tall, narrow door set into a hedge can provide a feeling of mystery and secrecy. An element of surprise can be pleasing; for example, entering through a gate onto a narrow path bounded by tall plants that suddenly turns a corner to open out and give a view of a wide-open garden. Or the gate itself can be the surprise; if you're handy with a saw, you can make your own unique gates from bought lumber or recycled wood. Whatever your choice, hang your gate from stout gate posts.

Some urban gardens have only a shady side entrance along a narrow strip between the house wall and the neighboring wall or fence. Even this small space can be made inviting, perhaps by painting your wall white to give off some light, covering the ground with pale gravel, and placing pastel-colored pots containing evergreens, such as camellias or azaleas, ferns, shade-loving perennials, or annuals along the edges. You could cover part of the passage with a wood pergola, attaching a horizontal wood beam to your own wall about 8 feet (2.5 m) above ground level and supporting cross members from that with posts of equal height on the other side. Then grow climbers from the ground or from containers to create a deliberately green, shady space, which then opens into a sunnier garden.

KEEP GATES IN SCALE

Watch the size of gates. A large but delicate gate can add drama to a small space, but a big, solid gate will dwarf a small garden and have little visual appeal.

A Variety of Gate Styles

A good gate can make a great garden. Depending on the size and style, it can add grandeur and mystery or make your space seem larger or more intimate. Choosing a gate should not be a last-minute decision; it will impact the atmosphere and overall feel of your garden, so incorporate your choice into the design as early as possible.

Door gates provide more security because they're tall. If you choose a delicate design, it adds a light touch.

Arched gate hedges are easy to maintain with proper support and a little pruning, but the area will look sparse during winter.

Ornate gates provide a beautiful focal point to large, manicured gardens, but they don't tend to look right with more rustic or homely spaces.

Modern gates can add a chic or fun element to your garden, depending on the design. These work well with minimalist spaces and clean lines.

Solid gates are very secure. They add an element of mystery to your garden, but they can block out light and might not be suitable for smaller spaces.

Setting Gate Posts in Concrete

Gates can take a lot of punishment, so make sure they are anchored firmly in the ground.

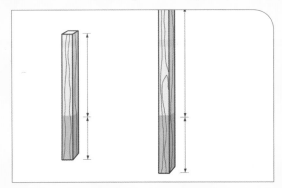

1 Wooden gate posts for a 3-foot (90-cm) gate need to be at least 18 inches (45 cm) longer than the finished height, to set them firmly into the ground. Gates taller than 4 feet (1.2 m) need to have posts at least 2 feet (60 cm) longer to set into the ground.

2 Dig a hole for each post (use a post digger if you can). Each hole should be about 9 inches (22 cm) wider than the posts, 22 inches (55 cm) deep for low gates, and 28 inches (70 cm) deep for taller ones. Put about 4 inches (10 cm) of gravel in the bottom of the hole for drainage.

3 Set the posts into the holes. Use a spirit level to check that posts are vertical and square, then brace them by nailing a length of 2 x 4 (5 x 10 cm) lumber to each post with its other end firmly on the ground.

4 Prepare concrete according to the package directions, or mix your own from one part Portland cement, two parts sand, and three parts fine gravel (aggregate). Add water until thick but not chunky. Wear gloves and a respirator mask so you don't inhale the cement dust.

5 Pour concrete into the trench up to ground level, check the level, and adjust the posts, if necessary.

6 Use a trowel to add some more concrete around the base of each post, making it mound-shaped. This will allow water to run off and not pool around the posts. Leave the posts to set for two days before hanging a gate from stout hinges.

INFORMAL AND FORMAL BOUNDARIES

Every garden needs something to mark the boundaries, for privacy, security, or just demarcation, and for protection from the elements. If you need privacy, choose evergreen or formal hedges, wood-panel fences or structures to support climbers. For protection you may need a thorny barrier, or just something to keep pests out—deer- and rabbit-proof fencing is a must in many country gardens. Or perhaps you need a windbreak (use a tall hedge, or an informal screen of shrubs and trees). If you inherit a garden with an attractive wall, consider yourself very lucky; walls offer all sorts of opportunities for climbing plants as well as protection, but they are expensive to build.

You might choose a hedge over a fence because it will last a lifetime and offer homes to birds and all sorts of other creatures. But hedges are not instant solutions in situations where privacy is an immediate need. A formal evergreen hedge can make a strong statement, but an informal hedge or screen of plants works well in many country gardens. An informal hedge can perhaps mix

MIXING CONCRETE

If you are mixing concrete for anchoring fence posts or a gate, you can hire a cement mixer or mix concrete with a shovel in an old wheelbarrow. But be sure to rinse all your tools thoroughly before the concrete dries.

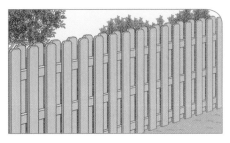

Board-on-board fences provide a secure boundary and require little maintenance.

Picket fences are picturesque but will need rubbing down and repainting every year or so.

Post-and-rail fences provide attractive boundaries for large areas.

20 Great Plants for Hedges and Screens

Clethra alnifolia, summersweet	*Nerium oleander*, oleander
Cotoneaster lucidus, hedge cotoneaster	*Picea abies*, Norway spruce
Deutzia gracilis, slender deutzia	*Prunus laurocerasus*, cherry laurel
Euonymus japonica, evergreen euonymus	*Pyracantha coccinea*, firethorn
Forsythia spp., forsythia	*Rhododendron* spp., azaleas
Hydrangea quercifolia, oakleaf hydrangea	*Rosa* spp., shrub roses
Juniperus spp., junipers	*Spiraea* x *vanhouttei*, bridal wreath
Ilex spp., hollies	*Syringa* spp., lilac
Ligustrum spp., privet	*Taxus* spp., yew
Lonicera nitida, box honeysuckle	*Thuja* spp., arborvitae

Erecting a Panel Fence

Panel fences are popular because they're easily available and quick to erect. Mix and match solid panels with trelliswork or lattice for climbers, or attach trellis above a solid fence to create a living fringe. Most panel fencing is made of pressure-treated, stained, or painted wood. Panels are often a standard size, and you can mix and match panels. Finish fences with a pressure-treated board that fits along the base to protect it from rot. Post tops should have wooden or ornamental caps. If your garden slopes, erect panel fencing with a stepped profile, so the panels will be upright, not slanted down the hill.

1 Clear the fence line of obstructions, then dig the hole for the end post. This will normally be at least 2 feet (60 cm) deep, and the width of your spade (or post hole digger). Use a spirit level to check that the post is vertical. Backfill with concrete (see page 37).

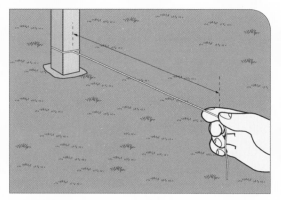

2 Run a line from the post to the end of the fence, stretching it taut. Panels are normally attached between posts, so measure the length of a panel from the edges of the posts, not the center, and dig the next hole.

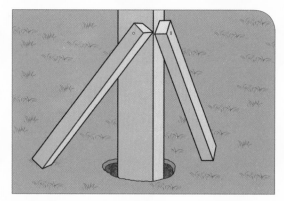

3 Set the second post in the hole, but don't backfill it. Either get someone to hold it, or brace it by temporarily nailing battens to the post that prop it in position.

4 Set the panel in position, checking that it is the right way up with the correct side facing out. Chock the panel up with blocks to give sufficient room for the base board. Attach to the posts as recommended by the manufacturer.

5 Cement the second post in position, and then repeat the procedure for the remaining length of fence. Never cement in the posts ahead of the panels, or you will have no way to correct any slight errors once the concrete sets. Finally, attach the base board and post caps.

evergreen hollies or rhododendrons with deciduous native plants, such as chokeberry, oakleaf hydrangea, clethra, or red-osier dogwood. A native hedge is a wonderful wildlife habitat as well as an attractive natural boundary. Avoid Leyland cypress hedges; they grow quickly into a dense, tall boundary, but they require a lot of maintenance once they reach the required height. In addition they don't support wildlife, and nothing will grow in their shadow.

PUT THE RIGHT SIDE OUT

The traditional way to set a fence is with the "good" side of the fence facing outward, toward the street, and the "back" side of the fence facing inward.

PATIOS

A well-made patio or deck beside the house is a wonderful thing—it's somewhere with a solid base where you can sit, soak up the sun, and entertain. It serves as a bridge between garden and house, and stops you from tracking dirt indoors on your shoes.

Size does matter. There's no point in having a patio or deck that's barely more than a strip by the door. Before you commit yourself to the hard work of laying a patio or building a deck—or having one constructed—take out a table and chairs and see if you can move comfortably around them. If not, the space is too small. If there's a problem paving around downspouts and the like, simply leave a small gap between the house and the paving and fill it with gravel.

The style of your patio depends largely on the materials you choose. They can blend in with plant foliage and other structures in your garden or they could make a sharp contrast to it. Reclaimed stone slabs and old bricks will give an instant sense of maturity to a garden. Small units, such as bricks, tiles, concrete pavers, and Belgian block allow you to make intricate patterns but can look very fussy in a large space. Slabs laid in rows running side to side across the yard make a space seem wider, while slabs laid running away from the house make a patio look longer. Random patterns can work well, but scale is especially important if you are using different-sized pieces. Include a selection of larger pieces with smaller ones for a large space, but keep the pieces small for a small patio.

If your ground is very sloping, go for wood decking with steps down to the garden rather than a patio. Decking is a versatile, low-cost solution to creating a flat outdoor space, and it is easier to construct than a patio.

Patio furnishings are best bought either in a good solid wood that can be rubbed down every year for longevity or quality plastic designed to be cleaned with a power wash.

MATCH LOCATION TO USE

Think about when you'll use your patio most. An east-facing patio or deck is lovely for sunny breakfasts but can be dismal late in the day. A west-facing patio or deck will catch the afternoon and evening sun. A south-facing one will be sunny all day and is great for sun worshippers, but you'll need plenty of shade in midsummer.

Patio Materials

There is a wide variety of paving materials available in local stores. Bluestone or sandstone are beautiful and durable, but old weathered ones can be even more attractive, if you can find them. Try salvage yards or put a small ad in your local paper or store.

Stone Slabs These make a stunning patio but are very hard to lay level because they will vary slightly in thickness. If they are not entirely level, they will frost-heave easily, making it hard to balance patio furniture.

Reconstituted Stone Slabs These are made from concrete but can look convincingly like real stone. They are the easiest to lay because they are uniform in depth and size.

Old Brick Old bricks are soft, absorbent, and slow to dry out. They can be slippery when wet but are good for small informal areas, perhaps mixed with slabs or Belgian block. They are not recommended for regions with harsh winters because they disintegrate after a few years.

Modern Brick Modern brick pavers are easy to lay and now come in interesting patterns, although they can look a bit too uniform for an informal garden. They need good, deep footings to prevent winter heave.

Poured Concrete For an alternative to the usual plain, grayish slab, you can have concrete that is textured, stamped, or stained with a pattern.

Cobblestones These stones are very attractive and ideal for details and patterns, but they are not easy to walk on or stand furniture on. They are lovely mixed with bricks or bordering slabs.

Belgian Block These blocks are expensive to buy and lay, and they look fussy over large areas. However, they are lovely for detailed work alongside bigger slabs. Recycled block is relatively easy to find.

Decorating a Patio or Deck

Furnish your patio with a table for dining and some comfortable deck or lounge chairs. If you have a barbecue grill, you may want a small table to hold spatulas and tongs and other cooking equipment.

Plants also add to the ambience of a patio. Hanging baskets of cascading and trailing plants are classic decorations for decks and patios. Hang them from brackets on walls or from stands with hooks. Hanging baskets are lovely in other places, too. Suspend them from a porch roof, place them near a door, or hang them from a lamppost.

SUMMER VACATION FOR HOUSEPLANTS

Many indoor plants will be happy spending summer outdoors on a deck or patio. Give light-loving plants morning sun, and keep medium-light plants in the shade. Water and fertilize as needed, and move plants back indoors when nighttime temperatures dip below 50°F (10°C) in the fall.

20 Fragrant Flowers to Grow near a Deck or Patio

Buddleia davidii, butterfly bush	*Lonicera* spp., honeysuckle
Ceanothus spp., California lilac	*Lathyrus odoratus*, sweet pea
Clethra alnifolia, summersweet	*Lavandula* spp., lavender
Dictamnus albus, gas plant	*Lilium* spp., lilies (many are fragrant)
Gardenia jasminoides, Cape jasmine	*Matthiola incana*, stock
Gelsemium sempervirens, Carolina jessamine	*Nicotiana sylvestris*, flowering tobacco
Heliotropium arborescens, heliotrope	*Paeonia* spp., peony
Hosta plantaginea, fragrant plantain lily	*Phlox paniculata*, summer phlox
Ipomoea alba, moonflower	*Rosa* spp., roses
Jasminum spp., jasmine	*Syringa vulgaris*, common lilac

DECKS

A deck is an attractive alternative to a patio, providing an appealing outdoor sitting space with easier installation and often at less cost. Decks have other advantages, too—you can easily create a level deck over uneven ground, and you can create a level space right outside a doorway where you might require steps to a patio. Alternatively, you could create a deck, like a balcony, leading from the first story of your house to take account of far-reaching views or to make extra outdoor space where you want to keep your garden for plants and play.

Decks are usually constructed of wooden boards, laid either straight or diagonally. They may be hardwood or softwood but must be treated in some way for durability. You can buy pressure-treated boards or choose untreated boards and treat them yourself with ecologically sound oils or varnish. You can stain or paint the boards; if you paint them, choose a strong marine varnish to seal them. You may need to sand the boards down and reoil or paint them after a few years' wear. Rot-resistant woods

20 Great Plants for Hanging Baskets

Alternanthera spp., alternanthera	*Lantana* spp., lantana
Begonia x *tuberhybrida*, tuberous begonia	*Lobelia erinus*, edging lobelia
Brachyscome iberidifolia, Swan River daisy	*Pelargonium peltatum*, ivy-leaved geranium
Browallia speciosa, bush violet	*Petunia* x *hybrida*, *P. integrifolia*, petunia
Calibrachoa or *Petunia*, million bells	*Sanvitalia procumbens*, creeping zinnia
Evolvulus pilosus, evolvulus	*Scaevola* x *aemula*, blue fan flower
Fuchsia x *hybrida*, fuchsia	*Thunbergia alata*, black-eyed Susan vine
Hedera spp., ivy	*Tropaeolum majus*, nasturtium
Helichrysum petiolare, licorice plant	*Verbena* x *hybrida*, garden verbena
Impatiens cvs., bedding impatiens	*Vinca major* 'Variegata', greater periwinkle

such as cedar, cypress, and redwood are ideal for decks. Composite boards made of recycled plastic are widely available and increasingly popular, because they do not need maintenance. However, they will not weather like wood, and they do splinter.

Keep your deck surface clean by brushing it frequently with a stiff broom and give the boards a thorough cleaning once a year in spring or fall. This will keep them from becoming slippery and keep the deck in good condition. Wooden decks also need to be painted or restained and waterproofed periodically.

Your deck can be unique; it can be almost any shape from rectangular to octagonal, high or low. If it is elevated, you may have steps in different styles and you will need railings, which can be plain or decorative. For safety's sake use a fireproof mat on a deck under a barbecue or outdoor heater.

Planks for a deck can be laid in various patterns—straight, diagonal, or herringbone, for instance.

Other considerations for decks are railings—elevated decks need them; you need to decide how high and what they should look like. Also do you want benches or built-in seating? Often benches can be built with hinged tops to allow storage underneath. If you want to have a barbecue, firepit, or outdoor heater, you will need a fireproof mat for underneath.

PATHS

For ease of navigation, make your main paths at least 3 feet (1 m) wide so you can comfortably push a wheelbarrow along them, or so two people can stroll side by side. For stability, paths should be laid on a solid base.

Other paths are for the pleasure of taking you on a journey around the garden. These are designed for dawdling and can be narrow, winding, and less substantial. An informal path can be as simple as a few stepping stones set into grass or as detailed as a decorative mosaic of tiles and cobblestones.

Brick Path Styles

Different styles of brick paths look best with certain types of garden. A straight and wide path with a running bond appears bold and formal, whereas a winding path in herringbone is more whimsical.

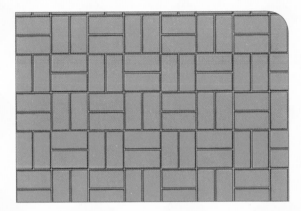

Basket Weave

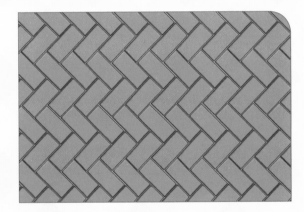

Herringbone

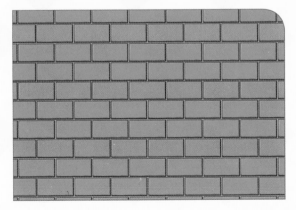

Running Bond

Path Styles and Materials

Stone slabs look handsome but are hard to lay except in straight lines. Brick paths look particularly attractive in country gardens, especially old recycled bricks where the odd crack can add to the charm. Modern concrete pavers that mimic the look of brick or stone are widely available. Gravel is popular because it's cheap and quick and easy to lay; the trick is to restrain it well with an edging. Cobblestones are lovely and fun to lay if you're patient, but it is slow work. A mixture of bricks and cobblestones in separate blocks works well, perhaps with tiles or pieces of stone combined.

Stepping stones or wood rounds sliced from a log may be all you need to cross a bed or an area of grass. A path of stepping stones is easy to install and perfectly suited to informal and naturalistic landscapes. You can use flagstones, bluestone slabs, or fieldstone to make a stepping-stone path. Just be sure the top surface of each stone is level with the soil surface so people don't trip. You can also set stepping stones in a base of pebbles, small gravel, or sand.

An instant or temporary path, especially in a woodland setting or a vegetable garden, can be covered with a mulch of wood chips, shredded bark, pine needles, or even straw or shredded leaves. You will need to add new mulch every year or two.

Making the Path

To prepare a path, first plot the course with stakes and string. Measure the width of the path every few feet to keep the width consistent. Excavate the path area several inches deep. Level the path area, and lay down landscape fabric to suppress weeds. If your path will be paved with loose stone, install an edging to hold the stone in place. Next spread a base of coarse crushed stone. Top that with a layer of sand, tamp it down or roll it with a lawn roller, and check that it is level. Then spread the top layer of gravel, pebbles, or other material.

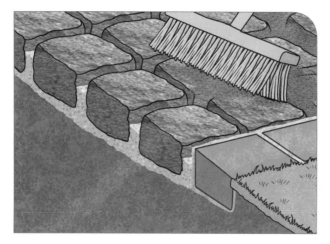

Cobblestones need a solid foundation; lay cobbles into a sand mix and brush dry cement mix in when finished. Pebbles will break away from the edge unless they are restrained, so edge with stone or brick, bedded on mortar. Use pebbles shaped like flat disks, cylinders, or blocks so that they can be packed tightly together.

PERGOLAS, ARCHES, AND ARBORS

Arches are a delightful way of passing from one part of the garden to another. You can train fruit trees together into living arches, or build arches from rustic poles or machined lumber, perhaps combined with sections of trelliswork or lattice. There are also arches crafted of wrought iron. Arches come in any number of styles, too—rounded or squared, rustic or elegant. Any type of arch you install will probably eventually be partially obscured by plants. Just make sure the structure is sturdy enough to support the plants you choose—some of the cheaper mass-produced arches just don't do the job for long. Rustic arches made from branches and woven twigs are charming covered with old-fashioned annuals, such as sweet peas, morning glories, or climbing beans.

Pergolas are longer walkways, sometimes with pillars of brick but usually made of lumber. They may be freestanding or have one side attached to a building. Beams should be supported by posts every 6 feet (1.8 m), or closer together if you want to grow heavy, woody plants, such as wisteria or laburnum. A pergola looks lovely when covered with wisteria or trumpet vine, perhaps interspersed with clematis and climbing roses. But while a pergola needs to be sturdy, it should be in scale with the landscape. You want to end up looking at a tunnel of plants, not at a daunting structure. A very substantial pergola can complement a large garden or a deliberately geometric garden design, but it will look out of place in a small or informal garden. Cover pergola uprights with flexible wire mesh or trellis to support vines as they grow. You can also cover the roof to provide increased support for climbers as well as added shade.

An arbor can make a wonderful shade over a sitting area or a secret space in a corner of your garden. An old-fashioned grape arbor over a patio will create a shady place for a picnic table or some comfy lounge chairs. Although pergolas traditionally formed shady walkways dividing different areas of the garden, in a small garden you can use one as a shady summer garden room.

WORKING WITH BENT WOOD

You can weave or bundle twigs or slender branches together to use in making a rustic arch or arbor. When you cut wood that you will bend into the shape you want, use it within an hour or so after you cut it, so the wood will still be pliable enough to bend without breaking.

Pergolas suit any style of garden. Small areas go well with simple shapes in treated wood, and more ornate gardens can take on a colonial feel with detailed pergolas painted white.

ROSE ARBOR SMARTS

Rose arbors are always popular. Be sure to fasten the thorny canes securely to the upright posts as they grow. There's nothing pleasant about having to untangle yourself from thorny stems. Scented jasmine or clematis are less hazardous bets for training over arbors.

Making a Wooden Pergola

If you want to add a shaded area to your garden, try a pergola. This wonderful structure can change the entire look of your outdoor space by giving it a Mediterranean feel. This simple plan is appropriate for most gardens, and more ornate designs for very large houses are available online. Although a pergola does not have a fully covered roof, it does give you the sense of a more intimate and cosy outdoor living area than a deck or patio that is totally uncovered.

It might look complicated, but even a DIY virgin can tackle a pergola. You just need to know how to cut the lumber. Use pressure-treated lumber or rot-resistant western red cedar that should last for years. Always check that whatever wood you buy comes from a sustainable source and has been treated for outdoor use. You can also stain the wood to match your garden color preferences, though this might need a reapplication every year or so, depending on how much sun your garden gets.

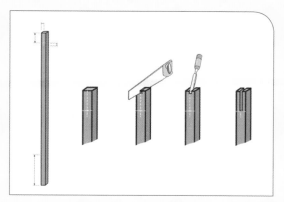

1 **Preparing the Posts** Mark a line 2 feet (60 cm) from the base of each post to mark ground level. Be accurate when setting the posts into the ground. Clearly mark a horizontal line 8 inches (23 cm) below the top of the post and a vertical line 2 inches (5 cm) in from the edge, extending 2 inches (5 cm) below the horizontal mark. Cut a 2-inch (5-cm) notch from the edge of the post between the marked lines by running a series of saw cuts 1 inch (2.5 cm) deep and then cleaning the notch out with a chisel. Notched beams will fit snugly into these rabbets and you then bolt them to the posts with ½-inch (12-mm) galvanized carriage bolts and washers.

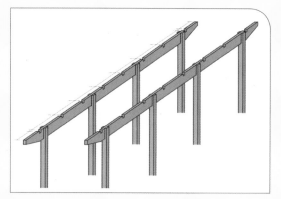

2 **The Beams** Cut two 2 x 8-inch (5 x 20-cm) beams 14 feet (4.2 m) long, tapering them at the ends, which will jut over the end posts by 14 inches (35 cm). On the top edge of each beam measure in 12 inches (30 cm) and mark it clearly, then measure an additional 2 inches (5 cm) along at 14 inches (35 cm) from the ends and mark this clearly. Make a 2-inch (5-cm) notch in between the two marks in the same way you made notches on the posts. Make similar notches along the tops of the beams on 20-inch (50-cm) centers; a total of 8 notches spread evenly along each beam.

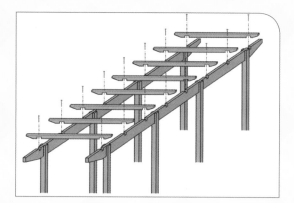

3 **The Crosspieces** Cut eight 2 x 3-inch (7.5 x 5-cm) pieces 64 inches (160 cm) long, tapering them at each end. Make two notches 2 inches (5 cm) wide and 1 inch (2.5 cm) deep on the bottom side of each rafter. These notches will line up with the notches on the top side of the beams. When you assemble them, you just tap the crosspieces firmly into place and nail through the top of each crosspiece with 3 ½-inch (9-cm) galvanized nails.

WATER FEATURES

Water is important in a garden, for the way it mirrors the sky above and reflects light and shadow, for the sense of serenity moving water brings, and especially for wildlife—even a sinkful of water will be full of insects within a few days, birds will love it and frogs usually find their way to it in no time, particularly in spring. Moving water that splashes or trickles brings music to the garden with its gentle sound, along with a feeling of coolness. Garden pools also offer an opportunity for all sorts of interesting planting—who can resist the idea of water lilies?

Set up a water spout to trickle gently in a quiet corner of the garden, or install a pool with a small fountain in view of your sitting area so you can catch the play of light upon water. It can be equally intriguing to hide it away so you hear the water but it is a surprise to come across. One reason to avoid water is if you have young children, because their safety must be a priority. But if you already have a pond on your property, try to find ways to make it safe before you get rid of it. You may be able to purchase a metal grid or wire netting cover, or you could surround the pool or pond with a fence with childproof closures, such as the ones sold to enclose swimming pools. Or you can drain the pool, make holes in the liner, fill it with manure and compost, and create a bog garden with plants such as cardinal flower and marsh marigold.

Any garden is large enough to accommodate a water spout coming out of a wall into a tub, or just trickling gently over a pile of stones. Easy to find and easy to install, a simple water feature will transform a hot garden and attract birds and other small creatures. A small fountain can be as simple as a gentle gush of water through a stone with a hole in its center into a disguised bowl or a tiny pool, to something much grander. All it takes is a nearby source of fresh or household water and the option to connect a pump to an electric supply to keep a pool fresh.

Types of Ponds

A traditional water feature, a pond has many possibilities that build on these basic designs.

A formal pool with paved, tiled, or raised surround can suit an informal garden as well as a formal one.

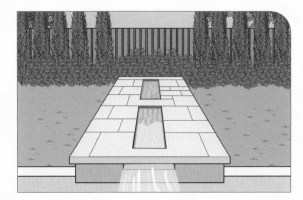

A rill is a straight channel of water leading to a pond, often edged with cut stone or tiles. It usually is laid on a slight gradient and water is pumped from the pond via an underground pipe to keep the water circulating from the top of the rill.

An informal pond with shallow edges for marginal plants is wonderful in a wilder area.

Constructing a Pool Using Flexible Liner

Building a pond from traditional materials (brick, cement, and clay) is very rewarding, but the process is time- and labor-intensive, requires a high level of skill, and is restricted to simple shapes. Flexible plastic liners allow you to create watertight ponds in more flowing and natural designs. They are widely available and very easy to install. The hard part, as always, is the digging.

POOL LINER SIZING

The width of a flexible pool liner should be the maximum pool width plus twice the maximum depth. The length of the liner is the maximum pool length plus twice the maximum depth.

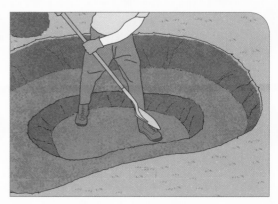

1 Dig the pool out to the required depth plus 2 inches (5 cm). If your pool is large enough to allow marginal planting, leave a shallow 12-inch (30-cm) shelf around at least one edge. Water lilies ideally need a depth of at least 3 feet (90 cm).

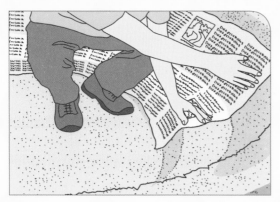

2 Line the sides, shelf and base with moist soft sand and a generous layer of newspaper. This prevents small stones from puncturing the liner.

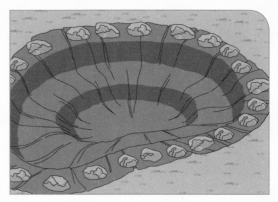

3 Lower the liner into position, weighting the edges with stones or bricks. Avoid stepping on the liner.

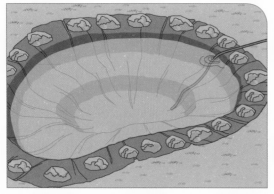

4 Fill with water.

5 Trim off the excess liner to leave 12 inches (30 cm). Then edge the pool with stone, bricks, tiles, or cobblestones laid on a pad of mortar.

20 Great Plants for Pools and Ponds

Acorus gramineus 'Variegatus', variegated Japanese rush	*Myriophyllum aquaticum*, parrot's feather
Canna 'Longwood Hybrids', water canna	*Nelumbo nucifera*, sacred lotus
Carex spp., sedges	*Nymphaea* cvs., water lilies
Colocasia esculenta, elephant's ear	*Pistia stratiotes*, water lettuce
Cyperus alternifolius, umbrella palm	*Pontederia cordata*, pickerelweed
Hydrocleys nymphoides, water poppy	*Sagittaria latifolia*, arrowhead
Iris ensata, Japanese iris	*Saururus cernuus*, lizard's tail
Iris pseudacorus, yellow flag	*Typha minima*, dwarf cattail
Iris versicolor, blue flag	*Vallisneria* spp., eelgrass
Marsilea quadrifolia, water clover	*Zantedeschia aethiopica*, calla lily

Plant a water lily in a tub

1. To plant a mature water lily plant with leaves (lily pads) and a stem, first fill a pot about 9 inches (22 cm) deep and 12 inches (30 cm) in diameter with potting soil or good topsoil (do not use potting mix, peat moss, or compost). Add a handful of bone meal for a hardy water lily or a handful of sand for a tropical one.

2. Work the plant gently into the soil, being careful not to damage the delicate roots. Set the tuber of hardy lily against one side of the pot, at a 45-degree angle. Position a tropical water lily in the center of the pot. The crown of either type of water lily should be above the soil surface. Topdress with a layer of sand or pea gravel, then water thoroughly.

3. Set the pot in a tub of water that has been allowed to sit for 24 hours so the chlorine can dissipate. There should be at least 6–8 inches (15–20 cm) of water above the soil surface at all times, and the leaves must not be under water. Set the pot on a brick if the water is too deep.

HARDY VS. TROPICAL WATER LILIES

Here's how to tell whether a water lily is hardy or tropical: The flowers of hardy water lilies (that will grow in a wide range of climates) float on the surface of the water. Tropical water lilies (that in all but the warmest climates are dug and stored for winter or grown as annuals) are carried above the water on thick stems, and many are richly fragrant.

Types of Edging Styles

Choosing an edge for your garden bed depends on cost and style. Stone costs more than wood, but it will last longer.

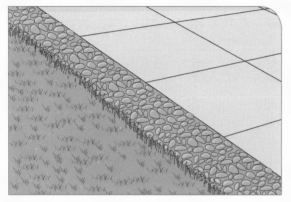

Line of stone between lawn and bed

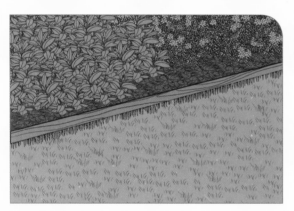

Line of timber between lawn and bed

Bricks or cobblestone against hard ground

BEDS

Beds provide the opportunity for adding color, texture, scent, and form through planting, and their shape is also part of the structure of the garden. Place them where you are going to be able to enjoy them the most—along sidewalks and paths, in front of and alongside the house, next to your deck or patio, or create island beds in a lawn. Beds can be geometric in shape—squares, rectangles, circles, triangles—or they can be gracefully curved ovals, ellipses, kidney shapes, or even free-form shapes. The only thing to keep in mind is that you will need to wield the lawn mower around them without too much trouble, if you choose very fancy shapes. Beds for permanent ornamental plantings can be any shape, but it's more practical to grow vegetables in a bed shaped for easy tilling and access—rectangles and squares are typically the most sensible.

Carving Beds Out of a Lawn

If you're creating beds where there was previously hard landscaping, you need to first remove all surface material. The soil beneath will probably be compacted so you will need to break it up with a pickax or mattock. Then dig or till it thoroughly. Add at least six spadefuls of well-rotted manure or garden compost per square yard (meter). You may also need to add new topsoil—make sure this is screened so you're not importing rocks and stones.

If you are removing turf to make a bigger bed or a new bed, it's a good idea to shake off as much soil as possible from a thin slice. Bury the rest of each piece of sod as deeply as you can rather than removing it, because it contains valuable nutrition. Or compost the sod before returning it to the garden.

Edging the Beds

Beds in grass look best when their profile is slightly separated from the grass. You can

Cutting Beds from Existing Lawn

Cutting your own flowerbeds is simple but hard work. Precision is key to make sure you get a clean edge between your lawn and the flowers, and this will also make maintenance easier with less grass invading the beds. All you need is a spade and a hoe, and because you're doing all the work yourself, any design is possible. Choose a flat piece of land for your new flowerbeds, and try to avoid digging after heavy rainfall. The sod will be easier to cut into neat lines when the lawn is a little dry.

1 Mark the outline of the bed with rope, sand, or landscape marking paint, then cut along that line to about 3 inches (8 cm) deep with a sharp spade.

2 Holding your spade almost flat to the ground cut under the sod you need to take out and remove it, taking no more than 1–2 inches (2–5 cm) of soil with the grass.

3 Break up the surface of the new bed thoroughly with a fork to get air into the soil.

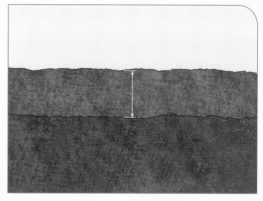

4 Cover it with at least 4 inches (10 cm) of well rotted-manure or compost and turn this organic material into the soil.

either do this by regularly cutting neat edges with a half-moon edging tool, or make permanent edgings from lumber, bricks, pavers, or stone to separate soil and grass and make the edges of the grass easy to cut. Straight beds are easily edged with boards. Just insert a board along the edge of the grass when you create the bed, level with the cutting height of the grass (use a spirit level to check the height). It will be held in place by the weight of the soil, so it should not need to be staked. Stone edging tiles, bricks or cobbles make attractive edgings, particularly where beds border a patio or driveway. Set them in concrete and mortar.

LAWNS

There's no argument that an expanse of cut grass in your landscape is a great companion to flowerbeds and trees and can be a wonderful way of defining spaces. The bright green, immaculately clipped lawn is not as popular as it used to be. These "perfect" environments require lots of time to maintain—they need mowing, fertilizing, and watering in dry spells. A lawn should be hard wearing and a place to relax, and it should not demand more than reasonably regular mowing. If you can't live with the occasional weed or rough patch, don't have a lawn. You might prefer to plant low-maintenance groundcovers instead.

If you do decide you want a lawn, choose grass that will cope with the amount of wear and tear you subject it to, and think about how often you want to mow (you may be someone who actually enjoys the process of mowing). It is also important to plant grass varieties suited to your climate and growing conditions. Some grasses need full sun, while others can tolerate shade. Some work best in northern climates and others grow well in warm southern gardens either in winter or summer.

Bypass all the chemical fertilizers and weedkillers on your lawn—they end up polluting waterways. You can use old-fashioned organic materials instead; they are widely available.

Landscaping with Grass

Grass doesn't have to be consigned to a garden backdrop; another approach is to use it as the principal landscaping material or the main canvas for exciting natural designs. You can cover an earth mound with grass to create living sculptures, mow patterns into it, or use it as a flowerbed in its own right by studding it with patterns of bulbs.

Sowing Seed for a Conventional Lawn

Sowing your lawn from seed is inexpensive compared to buying rolled sod, and you have a wider choice of grasses. The process is longer and more labor-intensive, but well worth the effort. Grass seeds need to be sown in spring or fall, and on damp soil. If the weather forecast predicts heavy rain or high temperatures, wait for more moderate conditions to plant your grass seeds. Climates that are hot or dry all year struggle to produce classic soft green grass, but some more hardy species like St. Augustine, Bermuda, zoysia, buffalo grass, and tall fescue fare very well in these areas.

1 Clear and thoroughly cultivate the area, adding a handful of well-rotted manure or compost every square foot (0.3 square meters) for a conventional lawn. Rake the soil to a fine tilth, leveling it as you go.

2 For a small area lay bamboo canes on the surface to form a few 3-foot (1-m) squares to make sure you are sowing the right amount of seed. Once you have sown a few squares, you will be able to judge how much to scatter.

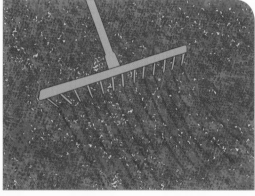

3 Lightly rake over the sown seed.

4 Water and make sure the grass seed bed does not dry out.

Laying Sod

For a manicured result in less time, laying sod is a good alternative to seeds. Before you purchase the sod, remember to check your soil's pH level with a store-bought or simple test (see page 69). For most grasses, if it's less than 6, then apply lime and test again; if more than 7.5, apply sulfur and test again until pH is correct. Spread a starter fertilizer and a soil conditioner onto the ground with a tiller before laying the sod—this helps to ensure that your prepaid lawn comes out perfect.

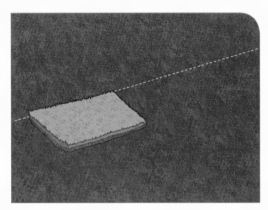

1 Start from a fixed point to lay the first sod against a straight edge.

2 Place a board over the laid sod and lay the next line in a staggered pattern, closely butting the edges and tamping each line down gently with the back of a heavy rake. This will seal the joints.

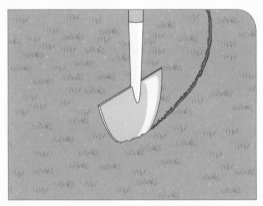

3 Move the board as you lay each line. Cut curves around edges with an old carving knife or half-moon edging tool.

4 If you need to fill any small gaps and joints, sprinkle sieved topsoil over them.

Naturalizing Bulbs Many spring bulbs and flowers will happily naturalize in grass. It often looks best to throw handfuls of daffodils and crocus from one spot onto the grass area so they fall in a natural drift and plant them where they fall. Deep blue scillas look wonderful planted in a wide band to get the effect of a river running across your grass in spring. Snowdrops, daffodils, crocus, and the lovely tall Spanish bluebell (*Hyacinthoides hispanica*) naturalize well in grass, and if you have a damp area, plant checker lily (*Fritillaria meleagris*). If they like their location, they'll spread quickly. Add to these with plugs of primroses. It's best to use spring flowers that have bloomed by mid-spring so that you can then give your grass an early summer haircut. If the grass grows too high, it can become difficult to cut and may turn into a mat that will stifle the flowers.

Labyrinth mowing creates an interesting pattern but requires a little skill and patience. Don't give up if it doesn't come out right on your first try.

Mowing Patterns Patterns cut in grass look very effective. Mark the pattern you want to cut on the ground with landscape marking paint, then mow it by setting the mower blades at different heights to contrast the textures of long and short. A simple checkerboard pattern is effective, or you can get more complex and mow a maze or a labyrinth.

Planting Bulbs in Lawns

Planting bulbs under the lawn is a low-cost, low-maintenance way to fill your garden with color in the spring.

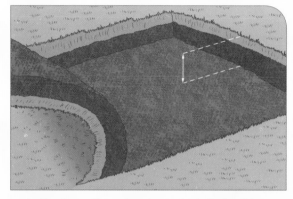

1 In October or November plant spring bulbs by slicing a hinged flap of turf between 2–3 inches (5–8 cm) thick.

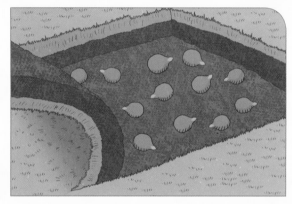

2 Scatter the bulbs on the bare soil.

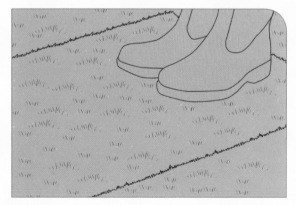

3 Replace the flap of turf and firm it gently by standing on it.

An Alternative to a Lawn

Wildflower meadows have become all the rage in the last decade. They are ideal for areas without huge wear and tear, because you only want to cut them a couple of times a year. A meadow can be a good option for an open, sunny area. Wildflower seed mixes are readily available, but don't be fooled by the picture on the packet. While your meadow area is establishing, weeds will also do their best to grow, and it can take several years to produce a good show. Some seed mixes contain lots of annuals that give you lots of color the first year and then disappear. Then the weeds really take over. Choose seed mixes containing native perennials suited to your region rather than imported varieties or annuals. But be prepared to do some weeding while the meadow gets established. A conventional lawn needs to be sown onto reasonably fertile soil, but a wildflower meadow can grow in average ground. If your soil is very fertile, try to remove the top few inches of soil and mix some sand into the seed bed. Once established, wildflower meadows are hard to beat and insects, birds, and bees will love the space as much as you will.

GROUNDCOVERS

For an area that doesn't get foot traffic, you can consider planting groundcovers. These low-growing plants don't need mowing, they're attractive, and many of them bloom. Some are evergreen and look good year-round.

20 Great Groundcover Plants

For shade	For sun
Alchemilla spp., lady's mantle	*Antennaria* spp., pussytoes
Asarum spp., wild ginger	*Cerastium tomentosum*, snow-in-summer
Chrysogonum virginianum, green-and-gold	*Chamaemelum nobile*, Roman chamomile
Epimedium spp., barrenwort	*Fragaria chiloensis*, ornamental strawberry
Ferns	*Juniperus horizontalis*, creeping juniper
Galium odoratum, sweet woodruff	*Phlox subulata*, moss pink
Lamium maculatum, deadnettle	*Sedum acre*, goldmoss sedum
Mentha requienii, Corsican mint	*Stachys byzantina*, lamb's ears
Pulmonaria saccharata, Bethlehem sage	*Teucrium chamaedrys*, germander
Tiarella cordifolia, foamflower	*Thymus* spp., thyme

UTILITY AREAS

The utility area is possibly the most important area in any garden; it's the functioning heart so ignore it at your peril. It needs to be somewhere accessible so that you do use it, and it probably needs to be screened from the rest of the garden. If you are lucky you'll have enough space for a compost bin or two, a tool shed, a cold frame or a greenhouse, as well as space to store a wheelbarrow, hose, bags of compost, and pots. You need an outdoor tap, and perhaps a rain barrel.

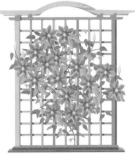

You should make space for a clothesline, whether a traditional affair strung between two posts or trees or a rotary dryer. If your garden is tiny you won't have room for a lot of stuff, but try to make room for a storage chest for a few handtools and gloves, even if it doubles up as a seat on a balcony, deck, or patio.

The site is crucial. If you tuck your utility area away somewhere uninviting, you'll never want to make the journey to the compost bin, and you'll probably end up leaving your wheelbarrow and tools somewhere in the garden or scattered around the basement rather than making the effort to put them away. Security is an issue in some gardens; don't put a garden shed somewhere it is too obvious to passersby, or too close to an obvious entrance or exit.

Screening Options

There are lots of ways to screen off the utility area. You can put up lattice panels or trelliswork and grow climbers on it. Or you could plant a hedge or a screen of plants. During the growing season ornamental grasses or a row of sunflowers or hollyhocks would screen the area, though they won't be there in winter. A high stockade fence would work, too.

Cold Frames

A cold frame is a great way to stretch your gardening season. It will allow you to keep slightly tender plants safe over winter and to start sowing seeds early. It's no more than a bottomless box with a glass or clear plastic lid to keep the frost off your tender plants or seedlings. Any sturdy box can be used as a cold frame; just cover the lid with a sheet of glass or Plexiglas. For a more professional look, construct a wooden box with a hinged front-opening lid. The box can be as large as you like, but a useful starting size is 18 inches (45 cm) tall and 18 inches (45 cm) deep, with a board along the front edge about 4 inches (10 cm) tall for the lid to rest on. You will need to fill in the ends with triangular pieces of board. For more information, see page 168.

Trelliswork with climbers is a good way to make simple screening for your garden.

If you have the space and are passionate about gardening, you may want to erect a greenhouse. A greenhouse should obviously be in a sunny spot, preferably with a water supply nearby. You want to catch as much south light as possible to ensure strong early growth, but it's fine to have your greenhouse partly shaded by deciduous trees; they won't block the light in early spring when young plants need maximum light but will give some shade from the intense midsummer sun.

GETTING DOWN TO EARTH

When you start a garden it's a natural reaction to want to get planting as soon as possible, but try and restrain yourself until you've tackled the soil. Plants, like us, need air, water, and food. Unlike us they can't move around to get what they need, but have to get all their nutrition direct from the soil they're growing in. So get down to the earth and get the conditions perfect from the start. Get your soil right now, and your plants will thrive.

You only need a few simple tools to get your soil into peak condition, but the key ingredient for this stage is patience. You'll need to assess your soil on a few key elements, such as drainage, pH level, and earthworm content. The instructions in this chapter take you through the process step-by-step, including the necessary remedies for deficiencies in your soil. Many beginner gardeners struggle to find the right balance for their gardens, often turning to harsh or expensive chemical treatments. Instead the methods described here are natural and easy-to-follow, though the occasional store-bought testing kit is sometimes useful.

GETTING TO KNOW YOUR SOIL

If you're keeping existing beds, rather than starting from scratch, it's tempting to assume all will be well, and if you're lucky it will be. But you really need to know your soil before you plant the first specimen. Once you know what you're working with, you can make sure you buy plants that suit your garden. Then you can set yourself up for easy gardening and prepare your garden for a healthy, flourishing future.

You'll need a few sensible tools to dig your soil when you start, and a good supply of compost, but otherwise you need little more than a basic understanding of what your soil is and does.

The type and quality of your soil depends on the underlying geology, your climate, and how well the soil has been maintained. Plant roots get air and moisture from the soil, and they also receive nutrients. Some plants also require specific types of soil in order to absorb the nutrients they need. It may all look like brown stuff to you, but plants can tell whether soil is alkaline, which is rich in lime, or acid, and which isn't. Some plants like one type, some need another. Rhododendrons and azaleas, for example, need acid soil, but lilacs and clematis prefer alkaline soil. The plants can also tell whether the soil is sandy or full of clay or rich loam, and they know whether it suits them or not. They'll soon tell you, too, and you'll quickly come to recognize when the plants are flourishing and when they're struggling.

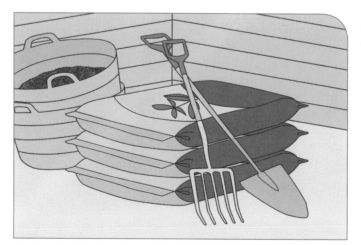

Packaged compost and fertilizer help restore organic matter to poor soil and support beneficial microorganisms.

60

SOIL—A NATURAL ECOSYSTEM

Soil is a natural ecosystem, which is self-sustaining when given plenty of organic matter. Plant leaves harness the sun's energy to manufacture carbohydrates from carbon dioxide in the atmosphere. They use carbohydrates plus nutrients from the soil to manufacture proteins and everything they need for healthy growth. When leaves and other organic matter fall to the ground they start to rot and become food for soil creatures, which convert it into more usable minerals to allow plants to grow more leaves. And the cycle continues.

All that we did, all that we said or sang,
Must come from contact with the soil.

—William Butler Yeats

The Carbon Nutrient Cycle

Carbon, calcium, nitrogen, and other fundamental nutrients travel from the soil and sun, into plants, and back into the soil and air through uptake, respiration, and decomposition.

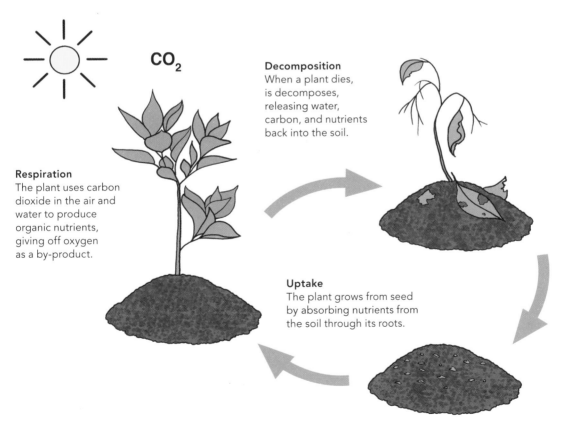

CO$_2$

Decomposition
When a plant dies, is decomposes, releasing water, carbon, and nutrients back into the soil.

Respiration
The plant uses carbon dioxide in the air and water to produce organic nutrients, giving off oxygen as a by-product.

Uptake
The plant grows from seed by absorbing nutrients from the soil through its roots.

Hang yarrow in your tool shed. This custom is based on herbal tradition; herbalists have long used yarrow to stop bleeding and would use it to treat garden injuries.

TOOL KIT

A few good tools will last you a lifetime so it's always worthwhile to go for the best you can afford and take good care of them. But if you're the kind of person who is not very good at putting things away or loses things, it may be better to start with cheaper tools and replace them once you realize your gardening bug is here to stay. But beware of silly tools. Garden centers are full of magic weed pullers, strangely shaped spades, forks, and prongs. Steer clear of them. The only essential tools you really need are a good spade, a fork, a trowel, a hoe, a pair of pruning shears, and a rake. If you have grass you also need a lawn mower and a springform rake. And for turning a lot of soil, you may want to rent or buy a rotary tiller or heavy-duty Rotovator.

You will use hand tools in the garden every day, so invest in some good ones that you'll want to look after. Copper trowels are beautifully shaped and lovely to use, and copper may help keep slugs off your plants—these trowels are too good to lose. Whatever type of trowel you buy, be sure it has a sturdy blade that won't bend and a strong handle. Flimsy trowels won't last long. You may find a hand fork useful, too.

A pair of good pruning shears is vital. Try them out before you buy to make sure they fit your hand well and that you like the action. Mark them with colored string or tape as soon as you get them home, or buy a pair with bright-colored handles so you can find them easily in the garden. Pruning shears have a habit of vanishing when you put them down in the middle of a pruning job.

A sturdy digging spade is another essential tool. Choose your spade carefully; some have longer handles than others, and some are more comfortable to grip. Make sure the handle is long enough for you; it should come to your hip bone. The best spades have wooden handles and stainless-steel heads that slice into the ground when you need to cut squares or dig trenches. If you treat a good spade right, it can last a lifetime. Most gardeners also like to have a shovel with a rounded or pointed blade on hand for scooping up compost and digging holes for plants.

In some situations, you need a digging fork. Where soil is dry and not too heavy, and where it has been dug before, use a fork. It breaks up clods better than a spade, aerates soil better, and is easier to push into the ground.

A rotary tiller or Rotovator is helpful if you have a large garden and need to break up a large area of really rough soil before digging in lots of manure and compost by hand. A Rotovator works much like a rotary tiller, but it is larger and made for heavy-duty work. The trouble with rotovating is that it breaks up every little weed root and can spread them around, leading to serious weed problems in the garden.

A good garden rake is useful for breaking up soil and creating crumbly seed beds. The thicker the head the better—thin heads can snap when they meet one stone too many on a rough bed.

CHOOSE A GOOD TOOL

Good-quality tools will last for years. Choose tools with sturdy handles (the classic wood for tools is North American white ash). The way the handle attaches to the metal working part of the tool is important. Look for tools with solid-socket, one-piece construction that completely surrounds the handle, rather than riveted attachments.

A wheelbarrow or garden cart is a versatile piece of equipment for even a small garden. If space is really tight, however, you may need to work with a plastic sheet and a plastic tub instead.

Whether or not you have an irrigation system or a hose hook-up, you will undoubtedly also need a watering can for spot watering. There are all sorts of watering cans, from cheap plastic ones to pricey metal ones, in many sizes. Whatever type you choose, just make sure it has a good rose that fits tightly and distributes water gently and evenly. Larger gardens usually need a hose; it is worth buying a good one that does not instantly tangle.

Essential Garden Tools

A good gardener needs to keep a small selection of specialized tools. While you might not use them all every week, having them on hand is better than running out to buy them at the last minute. If you have sensitive hands, try out a few different types of grips to avoid blisters.

Pointed shovel blade with D-handle

Flat-edged spade blade with T-handle

Tie coloured string to the handles of hand tools and pruners so you can see them when you leave them on the ground. You can also put some bright-coloured paint on the handles.

Trowel   Hand Fork   Pruning Shears

A flat-edged spade is better for precision digging a pointed spade is better for loosening ground, removing turf, or digging trenches. Tools either have D- or T-handles, and many shovels have long, straight handles; choose the more comfortable D-handle for digging tools. Long-handled shovels are more difficult to control when digging.

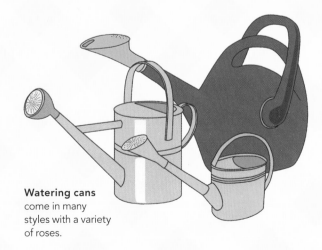

Watering cans come in many styles with a variety of roses.

KNOWING YOUR SOIL

You've probably never thought much about your soil, but once you know a little about how it is made up and what goes on underground, you can make sure that your soil always contains a good balance of plant food in conditions where plants can use it. Soil needs to be crumbly enough for worms to be able to move through it freely and spongy enough to hold moisture and air for plants to get the food they need.

TREAT YOUR ROOTS WELL

Plants get their nourishment through their roots, so you must provide them with rich, crumbly soil so that the roots can spread easily, and water and air can permeate the soil.

What Soil Is and What It Needs

Soil has been formed over thousands of years from the gradual breakdown of rocks and subsoil that erode and fragment through the action of water, ice, heat, and cold, and through chemical changes. Soil also contains decaying matter from plants and animals, plus air, water, and a mass of living insects, grubs, and microorganisms. Worms and insects drag organic matter from the soil surface deeper into the soil, and convert it into humus. Then soil bacteria, algae, and fungi get to work to release the nutrients from humus in a form plants can use—usable minerals, proteins, and carbohydrates.

Air gets into the soil via the passages made by earthworms and other burrowing creatures and in the water that drains through the soil. Water needs to be able to enter the soil and drain slowly for plants to use it. Plants get food in solution through their roots; if there isn't enough water in the soil they can't absorb enough nutrients. But if the soil is too wet the plants can't absorb the air they need, and they drown.

Soil profile

The soil profile refers to layers within soil. There are a few sub-classifications, but generally your soil will divide into a top, middle, and bottom layer—each with a specific purpose for the plants in your garden.

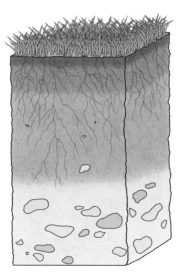

Humus, mature compost, or topsoil, is the fine, top layer of your soil rich in nutrients and life.

The next layer is subsoil, which is rich in minerals but not in humus.

Weathered rock and bedrock make up the lowest layer, with little plant or animal life.

If you have a lot of earthworms in your garden, you have good soil.

The structure of the soil determines the way it converts and stores food for plants. If it's too dense and full of clay, air and water won't be able to enter it evenly, organisms won't be able to do their job, and roots won't be able to get the food they need. If the soil is too loose and sandy, then air, water, and nutrients simply drain through the gaps and roots have nothing to grasp onto. Happily, whatever kind of soil you start with can be improved.

Recognizing Different Soil Types

When you begin a garden, the first step is to identify your soil type. The three main types of soil are sand, clay, and loam. They have different qualities because they are made of different-sized crumbs of minerals.

Sandy soils have large crumbs, which means they don't stick together closely and there are big spaces between each crumb. Sometimes called light soils, they are very easy to work but harder to keep in good condition because they tend to drain fast. Moisture passes quickly through sandy soils, taking nutrients with it. If you pick up a small handful and try to roll it into a ball in the palm of your hand, it will feel gritty and refuse to stick together.

The Earthworm Test

Earthworms are your soil's best friends—one worm can swallow and process between 20–200 tons (18–181 tonnes) of soil per acre (hectare). Take a worm count to determine the state of your soil life.

1 Dig a 1-foot (30-cm) square hole about 6 inches (15 cm) deep and place the soil in a shallow tray.

2 Count the number of earthworms in the tray.

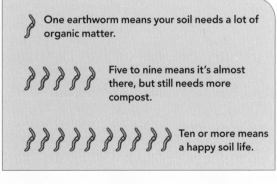

One earthworm means your soil needs a lot of organic matter.

Five to nine means it's almost there, but still needs more compost.

Ten or more means a happy soil life.

3 Use the above scale to assess the amount of organic matter in your soil.

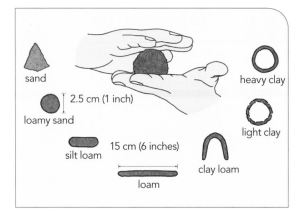

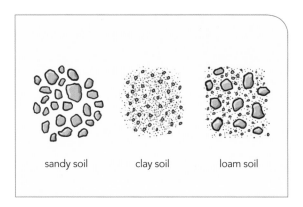

Roll a small amount of soil in your palm and match it to one of the images above to decide which type of soil you have.

Clay soils are made of tiny mineral crumbs which stick together like glue. Also called heavy soils, they are dense and hard to work, and difficult for air and water to penetrate. Clay soils can get waterlogged and airless, but they do hold nutrients well. If you can roll a handful of your garden soil into a sticky ball with a shiny surface when you rub your thumb over it, you've got clay.

Loam soils are a mixture of large and small crumbs, and are the gardener's ideal soil. Loam is crumbly and easy to work but holds air, water and nutrients well. You can make a soft, dark ball from a small handful of loam.

LIME IMPROVES CLAY

Adding ground limestone to clay soil helps the tiny clay particles bind together to form larger particles, helping to open up and lighten the texture of the soil.

IMPROVING SOIL

There is one magic ingredient that improves all soils – compost, well-rotted organic matter. Homemade compost is the best of all, but it's almost impossible to make as much as you need. You can supplement your own compost with manure or purchased compost from a garden centre. It is available in bags, and many nurseries also sell it in bulk by the yard. Some municipalities have composting operations and make compost available to residents.

If you have a heavy, clay-based soil you need to open it up so air and water can penetrate it and to improve its drainage. You need to dig in sand to improve aeration, and add well-rotted organic matter to support the soil life. Make sure the compost or manure you add is really well rotted or you can make matters worse, because the soil may not contain enough organisms to break down anything tough. If you have sandy soil, make it less gritty by adding a few centimetres of organic matter regularly.

COMPOST HELPS ALL TYPES OF SOIL

In clay soil, compost helps open up space between the tightly packed clay particles, allowing better penetration of air and water. In sandy soil, compost soaks up water like a sponge and helps hold moisture and nutrients in the soil longer.

The Jar Test for Soil

Another way to determine your soil type is to scoop a trowelful of soil into a glass jar. Fill the jar nearly to the top with water, screw on the lid, and shake well. Then watch as the particles settle out. Pebbles and bits of stone will sink first, followed by sand. Silt particles will settle out next, then clay. Some very tiny clay particles may stay suspended in the water. Particles of organic matter will settle on top of the clay or float. The relative quantities of the different particles will give you a rough idea of your soil's composition.

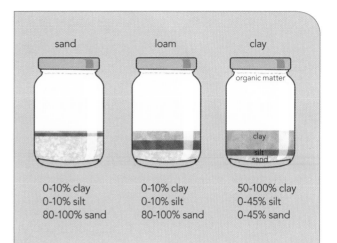

sand	loam	clay
0-10% clay	0-10% clay	50-100% clay
0-10% silt	0-10% silt	0-45% silt
80-100% sand	80-100% sand	0-45% sand

THE NUTRIENTS IN YOUR SOIL

Plants get most of their major nutrients from soil. The most important are nitrogen (N), phosphorus (P), and potassium (K). Nitrogen is essential for leaf and stem growth, and photosynthesis. Phosphorus is vital for cell division, root development, and the ripening of seeds and fruit. Potassium is vital for flowering, fruiting, photosynthesis, and uptake of other elements. The level of acidity or alkalinity, or pH, which is based on the concentration of hydrogen ions in the soil, is also important. The pH can affect the ability of plants to absorb and process other elements in your soil. In soils with a high pH, for example, phosphorus, iron, and manganese become less available.

Measured on a numerical scale of 1 to 14, a pH of 7 is neutral. Each number on the scale represents a pH 10 times lower or higher than the number below or above it. Numbers below 7 indicate acidity, and numbers above 7 indicate alkalinity. Alkaline soils often contain a lot of calcium. Most plants grow happily in soils between 6 and 7, and most soils fall somewhere between 5 and 8.5. But some plants, such as azaleas and rhododendrons, need acid soils, and some, like baby's breath and corydalis, prefer alkaline conditions.

One way to check pH is to buy an inexpensive test kit from a garden center. It's a good idea to take samples from different parts of your garden and determine the differences between them. You can't change a really acid soil to alkaline or vice versa, but you can keep neutral soils in balance. Organically cultivated garden soils are rarely too alkaline because regular applications of compost and other organic matter keep them in balance. If your soil is too acid—pH below 6—you can bring up the pH by one point by topdressing with about 5 pounds (2 kg) of ground limestone per

When testing soil in a jar use a marker to note the level of each layer as they settle one by one. Even if the soil mixes together again, you'll have the pen marks to use as a guide.

Not every soil can bear all things.

—Virgil

Plants That Indicate Soil Type

Wild plants can offer clues to soil type. If you see several of these plants in an area, they may indicate your soil type.

Sandy	*Lychnis flos-cuculi*, meadow pink	*Hieracium* spp., hawkweed
Centaurea cyanus, bachelor's button	Mosses	*Juniperus virginiana*, red cedar
Lactuca pulchella, arrow-leaved wild lettuce	*Polygonum persicaria*, spotted knotweed	*Leucanthemum vulgare*, ox-eye daisy
Linaria vulgaris, yellow toadflax	*Rumex acetosella*, sheep sorrel	Mosses
Lychnis alba, white campion	*Solidago canadensis*, Canada goldenrod	*Polygonum persicaria*, spotted knotweed
		Plantago major, plantain
Clay	**Humusy, Well Drained**	*Quercus ilicifolia*, scrub oak
Plantago major, plantain	*Amaranthus retroflexus*, pigweed	*Taraxacum officinale*, dandelion
Ranunculus repens, creeping buttercup	*Arctium lappa*, burdock	*Vaccinium* spp., wild blueberry
Rumex obtusifolius, broad-leaved dock	*Chenopodium album*, lamb's quarters	**Alkaline**
Taraxacum officinale, dandelion	*Cichorium intybus*, chicory	*Anthemis nobilis*, chamomile
	Portulaca oleracea, purslane	*Chenopodium intybus*, chicory and *Daucus carota var. carota*, Queen Anne's lace, together
Wet, Poorly Drained		
Acer rubrum, red maple	**Acid**	*Chenopodium* spp., goosefoot
Carex spp., sedges	Cresses	*Silene latifolia*, bladder campion
Eupatorium purpureum, Joe-pye weed	*Fragaria vesca*, wild strawberry	*Stellaria media*, chickweed

SOIL PROFILES ACROSS THE UNITED STATES

In general, parts of the United States where open land is (or was) covered with forests and there's plenty of rainfall, particularly the Pacific Northwest and the East, have moderately acid soils. Across the Midwestern prairies, where there is less rain and most natural vegetation is grasses and wildflowers, soil pH is close to neutral. In the arid Southwest, soils are generally alkaline, to the point of being salty in desert areas.

100 square feet (30 sq m) in sandy soil, 7–10 pounds (3–4.5 kg) in loam soil, and 7–8 pounds (3–3.5 kg) for clay soil. If you want to grow acid-loving plants but have a neutral to alkaline soil, you need to build raised beds or use containers and fill them with topsoil or potting mix with an acidic pH.

Correcting an Imbalance of Nutrients

For most gardens, correcting pH and spreading compost or manure each year will maintain adequate levels of nutrients in your soil. But sometimes the leaves of your plants can look sickly, pale, or discolored, you may need to give them a tonic.

Nitrogen Nitrogen is probably the most important nutrient of all. Plants need it for healthy, green foliage. And if they're not getting enough of it their leaves don't grow to normal size, the whole plants tends to be stunted, and the foliage is pale and yellowish rather than bright green. Luckily nitrogen deficiency is really easy to cure—just add livestock manure and compost or

pH scale

pH 4–5 Strongly acid
Found in cold, wet areas
Suitable plants: Camellias,
rhododendrons, heathers, azaleas,
blueberries, and cranberries.

pH 5–6 Fairly acid
Occurs in unimproved soil in
wet areas
Suitable plants: Magnolia,
potatoes, tomatoes, rhubarb,
strawberries, and celery.

pH 6–7 Neutral
Typical garden soil
Suitable plants: Most plants and
garden crops thrive.

pH 7–7.5 Alkaline
Found in dry and hot dry areas,
or where the underlying rock
is limestone
Suitable plants: Many garden
plants; cowslips, lilac, pinks,
cyclamen, brassicas, spinach.

dried blood, cottonseed meal, fish emulsion, or
bonemeal fertilizer.

Inorganic nitrogen-providing fertilizers
are usually based on ammonia, which harms
or drives away earthworms and can damage
other soil organisms as well. In addition, excess
nitrogen not absorbed by plant roots eventually
finds its way into the water table and can cause
pollution. It's better to use natural fertilizer
because it gets into the soil and stays there,
releasing its nutrients slowly over a long period.
Chemicals products offer a quick fix, but it is
easy to use too much or too little.

Phosphorus If the leaves on your plants
are small, pale, slow to open, and then fall
early, your soil may be lacking phosphorus.
Phosphorus deficiency is common in

Instant Rough pH Gauge

Before you buy a prepackaged kit, here is a simple
way to test if you soil is very alkaline or very acidic,
using only materials from the kitchen pantry.

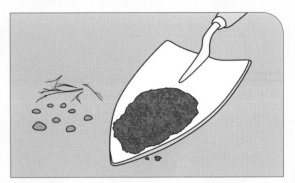

1 Dig up a handful of soil. Remove pebbles and large bits
of plant debris. Let the soil dry.

2 With a large stainless-steel spoon scoop up a tablespoon
of the dry soil. Add several drops of vinegar. If it makes
your soil fizz, your soil is alkaline.

3 Scoop up another spoonful of soil and add water until
it's completely moist. Add a pinch of baking powder. If it
fizzes, your soil has a pH less than 5.5 and is very acidic.

waterlogged soils, because phosphorus doesn't move easily in soil water. To improve drainage, add either sand or organic matter to improve the soil structure, or lay a few pipes in the ground for underground drainage. Then add compost, and dress with rock dust (ground rock phosphate or colloidal phosphate) or bonemeal in the autumn.

Potassium Potassium-deficient plants also have pale leaves and stunted growth, and leaves tend to be brown-tipped with yellow markings between the veins. Leaves may be spotted and curled, and stems weak. These plants need potash, so you can give them a dressing of wood ash from your woodburning stove or fireplace, as long as the wood you burned was not pressure-treated. Other organic sources of potassium include granite dust, greensand and seaweed meal.

If leaves are green but veined with yellow between the veins, be sure to water the plants with Epsom salts. Or add homemade compost. If the young leaves of iron-deficient plants are yellow between the veins, they also need compost or dressing with sulphur to reduce pH.

Instead of adding individual ingredients to supply nutrients for particular plants, it's often just as effective and more convenient to use an organic all-purpose fertiliser, which should solve your problems. The best idea is always to feed the soil rather than individual plants. If specific problems do occur, you can find specifically formulated mixes for flowers, trees and shrubs, roses, bulbs, acid-loving plants, vegetables, lawns and most other needs.

The 16 Elements Plants Need

Plants need these nutrients from soil or fertilisers, in varying amounts, for good growth:

Major Nutrients	Micronutrients (Trace Elements)
Nitrogen (N)	Boron (B)
Phosphorus (P)	Chlorine (Cl)
Potassium (K)	Copper (Cu)
Secondary Nutrients	Iron (Fe)
Calcium (Ca)	Manganese (Mn)
Magnesium (Mg)	Molybdenum (Mo)
Sulphur (S)	Zinc (Zn)

Plants also need carbon, hydrogen, and oxygen, which they get from air and water.

HOME COMPOSTING

All gardeners used to make compost; there was a time when waste had to be recycled because there was nothing else to do with it. Nowadays we can choose to have our waste taken away to landfill sites. We tend to not think about the amount of garbage we produce because we don't have to deal with it ourselves. But everyone should recycle what they can, and gardeners can recycle more than most. Almost anything that was once plant or animal matter can be composted and returned to the soil, providing food for new generations of plants and animals.

Compost is the best organic material you can give your garden, it promotes soil health, and healthy soil makes for healthy plants. Best of all it's free and easy to make. It is a mixture of natural materials, such as weeds, grass clippings, garden waste, and kitchen scraps. Throw these together in a heap or trash can and they will decay into a dark, crumbly, sweet-smelling mass to improve your soil and provide a balanced diet for your plants.

Ways to Apply Fertilizers

You can spread fertilizers to small, targeted areas (watering, side dressing, and slow-release pellets) or evenly to large areas (banding, broadcasting, and foliar feeding).

Watering is used to distribute fertilizer over small, targeted areas.

Banding is used on larger areas to distribute fertilizer.

Side dressing is a method of applying fertilizer to small, targeted areas.

Broadcasting is used to distribute fertilizer on larger areas.

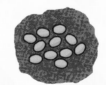

Slow-release fertilizers are used on small areas.

Foliar feeding is used on larger areas.

You don't need a huge garden in order to make compost. You can compost kitchen scraps in a worm bin on a balcony. You can be a lazy composter and just throw everything into a heap or a bin and leave it, or you can enthusiastically turn your compost regularly and speed the decomposing process. You can have usable compost in six months or less if you turn the pile regularly. An unattended heap usually takes around a year to break down.

Making Compost

Composting is not an exact science; there's a good deal of trial and error. You need the right balance of carbon (dry or brown) and nitrogen (wet or green) materials. If there's too much nitrogen in the pile, the excess is given off into the air as ammonia. If there's too much carbon in the pile, decomposition

Various Types of Compost Bins

A free-standing compost heap is adequate, but a bin will retain the water and moisture needed for decomposition, giving you better quality compost in less time.

Wooden bins retain water and moisture needed for decomposition.

Composter bins are typical in many gardens.

Tumblers are used as free-standing compost bins.

Plastic trash cans can also be used for composting.

will be slower. Just fill your bin or heap with a reasonably balanced mixture of about two thirds fibrous (brown) material to one third of soft (green) material. Fibrous material includes stems and twigs, straw, dried leaves or weeds, and roots. Soft materials include flowers, grass, and weeds as well as fresh livestock manure. You may prefer to compost fall leaves separately, because they take longer to break down if not shredded first.

Build your compost pile by laying down alternating layers of dry and wet materials. Keep adding material as you get it until the pile is about 3 feet (1 m) high and 3 feet (1 m) wide. When the pile is built, keep it moist but not soggy. Water it if the weather is dry, so it does not dry out.

Building a Simple Mesh Bin

A wire-mesh bin is simple to make and handles a good amount of material. You need 15 feet (5 m) of 2-foot-wide (60-cm-wide) wire-coated mesh fencing, flexible wire ties, and a pair of pliers.

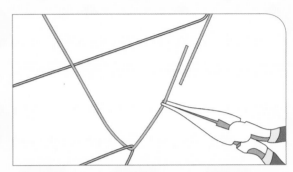

1 Cut five 3-foot (90-cm) sections of wire mesh. Use pliers to bend over and clamp each wire end flush to the mesh.

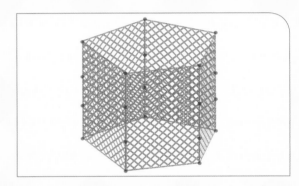

2 Attach the long edges of each panel to the next to form a pentagon. Tie each edge at the top and bottom and in two places in between.

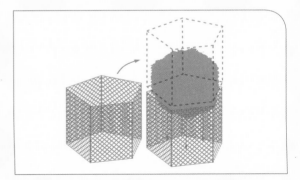

3 Find or create a site large enough to fit two bins side by side. To turn and aerate your compost, tug the bin up and off the pile, place the now-empty bin next to it, and refill it with the mixed compost.

An easy way to improve and protect your soil's fertility is to use mulch. It's not only good for suppressing weed growth, but mulching is the easiest way to add organic matter. Mulch helps slow the evaporation of moisture from soil in the summer, and helps prevent frost heaving in winter. Just spread the mulch on top of the soil and let worms and other soil creatures do the work to incorporate it into the soil.

You should only mulch when your soil is fairly wet, because rainwater will trickle very slowly through a thick layer of mulch. But the soil beneath the mulch won't lose much moisture and should stay moist even in very hot weather. Unless you are using the no-dig method, be sure to fork in or rake off excess winter mulch a few weeks before spring planting to let the soil warm up, and wait to remulch until plants put out new growth. You can use straw, hay, or evergreen boughs on light soil for a winter mulch to prevent erosion and as a good insulation from the thawing and freezing that harms less hardy plants. Don't mulch clay soil over winter—it needs to be as open to the elements as possible.

Organic mulches break down over time and need to be replaced or replenished from time to time. Just add a fresh layer of mulch on top of what's already there.

Green Manures

Green manures, or cover crops, are living mulches that are grown to improve the structure and nutrient content of the soil. A green manure will prevent soil erosion, bring nutrients closer to the surface of the soil, and boost soil nutrition when the crop is turned into the soil. Living mulches also attract insects and birds. White and red clovers, peas and beans, ryegrass, vetch, alfalfa, and some mustards are all good cover crops. Plant them in early spring or after the last harvest in late summer or fall, and till or dig them under about a month before planting the next crop.

ORGANIC FERTILIZERS

Gardeners should try to feed the soil, not the plants, but at peak growing times plants could also use a direct feeding with liquid fertilizer. You can buy specific liquid feeds. However, if you have space, make your own comfrey or nettle teas by steeping leaves in a trash can of water for four weeks or so and drawing off the liquid, which is full of nutrients. But beware, this smells truly awful so don't use it on houseplants! Another traditional fertilizer for roses and the vegetable garden is made by steeping a bag of muck (these can be purchased from stables) in water for a couple of weeks. Again, it doesn't smell too good but plants love it.

Organic materials and natural fertilizers release their nutrients slowly so plants can take them up when they need them, not when the gardener decides to dose them. If you do decide to dose your plants with a nonorganic fertilizer, such as 5-10-5 for a quick fix, follow the package directions for application, and remember that these products release their nutrients quickly and don't last long.

MULCH DEFINED

Mulch is simply a layer of material laid down over the surface of garden soil.

INVITE BIRDS TO THE GARDEN

Leave soil bare for a few weeks in fall before spreading winter mulch so birds can grub through your soil for pests, pest eggs, and larvae.

Different Mulches

Laying mulch is an excellent way to control weeds and clear ground. The mulch prevents any light from reaching the soil, helping to prevent unwanted sprouts.

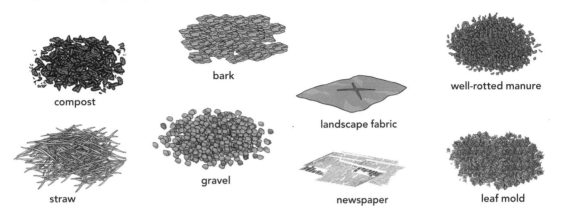

Compost—the best all-around mulch for weed prevention, insulation, protection, and nutrition.

Bark—use composted bark directly on the garden and fresh bark chips on top of landscape fabric as decorative mulch in nongarden areas.

Landscape fabric—excellent weed suppression, use before planting and make x-shaped slits to plant through.

Well-rotted manure—excellent protection and nutrition but never use on clay soils in winter.

Straw or hay—good insulation and nutrition but can cause increased weed problems as seeds germinate.

Gravel—use as a weed and slug preventive on small ornamental gardens and pots.

Newspaper—use thick layers and cover with bark or compost for best effect.

Leaf mold or shredded leaves—excellent for weed prevention, water penetration, and nutrition.

Making Compost or Manure Tea

An organic liquid feed is easy to make using homemade compost or manure, and it can be watered onto plants to give them a quick boost.

1 Put several shovelfuls of compost or manure into a burlap sack and tie it shut. Place the bag in a plastic bin or rain barrel and fill with water.

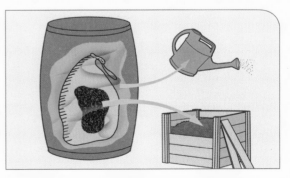

2 Let the "tea" bag steep for about three weeks. Remove it and toss the contents into the garden. Use the liquid to water plants, diluted to half strength if it is very dark in color.

When birds fly high in the sky, the weather will be good.

Raised beds can be made from pressure-treated lumber (as shown below), railroad ties, bricks, or stone.

HOW AND WHEN SHOULD I DIG?

Most people think that all gardening requires regular digging. Not so. In a well-managed garden you should only need to dig the soil once, right at the beginning. You dig to break up the soil and loosen it so air, water, and roots can penetrate and to add organic matter to improve its fertility. You'll need to continue to add organic matter, but you can add this as a mulch or fork it in as you weed or add more plants. As you dig, you weed, but digging is different from weeding, which needs to be done regularly to be effective. A well-dug patch should be relatively weed free.

Single (ordinary) digging just involves turning over the soil to take off weeds, break down clods, and add manure or compost. You may find it easiest to use a fork except in heavy soils where you'll need a spade.

You can decide on your digging options by digging a hole about two spade or shovel heads deep. If the soil is reasonably loose in the bottom half, you only need to dig one spade deep. But if the soil is compacted at the deeper level you need to loosen it for drainage and aeration by double digging. This procedure involves turning over the subsoil as well as the topsoil and adding organic matter to each level. The easiest way is to divide your plot into 18-inch (45-cm) squares. Take out a shovelful of topsoil from the first and second squares and a shovel of subsoil from the first square and leave these to one side. Then turn the subsoil from the second square into the first, adding compost or manure, and cover it with weeded topsoil from the third square. Repeat the procedure to work your way across the bed. Soil from the first squares will go into the final pair.

NO-DIG GARDENING AND RAISED BEDS

The principle of the no-dig technique is to leave a thick layer of well-rotted compost covering the surface of your soil and to keep renewing it each year. Some gardeners never even dig their ground at the beginning. But you need to think ahead if the no-dig method is your strategy, because your future growing area will be out of action for at least one growing season.

The first step is to mow grass and chop down weeds on the area you want to turn into a bed. Then spread a layer of cardboard or several layers of newspaper on the ground. This covering excludes light to stop weed seeds from germinating, and it will eventually rot into the ground. On top of this spread a 4-inch (10-cm) layer of compost or well-rotted manure or leaf mold, then another layer of cardboard or newsprint, and finally cover this with another thick layer of compost. Keep everything damp so the living organisms in the soil can get to work breaking down all the organic matter. You should be able to plant after about six months if your growing season is long enough; otherwise, wait until next year. Add another inch (2.5 cm) of compost and plant in that.

Raised beds are best if your soil is very poor, if it is any way contaminated, or if you want to grow acid-loving plants in an otherwise alkaline environment. They are ideal for no-dig gardening; just fill them at the beginning and keep topping them up with compost. You can make raised beds by simply mounding up the soil and sloping the sides or contain the soil with railroad ties (use ties intended for landscaping, which have not been treated with creosote). The ties are wide enough to act as seats as well as edging. Or contain raised beds with rot-resistant wood planks at least 6 inches (15 cm) by 1 inch (2.5 cm), or with cement blocks. Brick or stone raised beds work well in ornamental gardens and in herb gardens, and they are ideal for gardeners whose mobility is limited.

When you've made the framework for the bed, fill it with a mix of topsoil and compost or leaf mold or manure, or a special ericaceous soil mix if it's for acid-loving plants. What you use depends on what's easy to find. If you have ready access to topsoil, use a blend of 80 percent soil and 20 percent compost. However, if access is a problem, you may just use compost and rotted manure laid over the existing earth. It's not worth using small bags of expensive topsoil for anything much larger than a windowbox.

A GOOD BED FOR SEEDS

To create a good bed for seeds, dig or till the soil, water well, then let the soil settle until the surface is dry enough to work (a ball of soil squeezed in your hand will crumble when you open your fingers). Then rake until the soil has a fine texture like coffee grounds. Smooth and level the surface.

Sheet Composting

Also known as passive composting, this process requires minimal labor. Results take time, but it allows you to reclaim land to create fertile gardening sites.

1 Cut any plants growing on the site, and then cover the area with sheets of cardboard and newspaper.

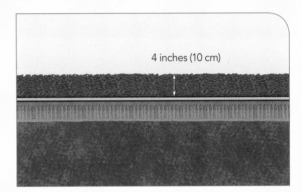

2 Cover the cardboard and newspaper with manure and layer plant materials on top. Compost needs carbon-rich materials (dead leaves) and nitrogen-rich materials (grass clippings) to work really well.

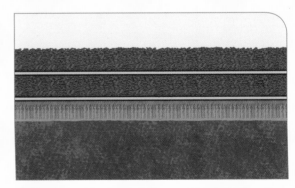

3 Continue adding layers until you get the desired result. Do not use wood chips or other materials that take a long time to break down.

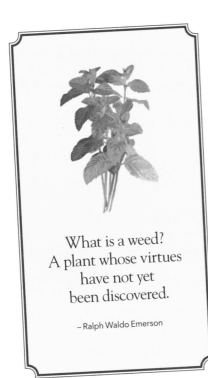

What is a weed?
A plant whose virtues
have not yet
been discovered.

– Ralph Waldo Emerson

WEEDING

Weeds are often described as being plants in the wrong place. Some gardeners love to see clover and buttercups in their grass, others get positively neurotic about them. Many annual weeds are very attractive and most can be removed easily, but perennial weeds can be vicious. You need to get rid of them or they will smother plants that you really do want.

You'll have to weed from time to time, so learn to love it. Think of weeding as a way to get to know exactly what is in your garden, to check the progress of every plant, and enjoy really noticing every new flower or every plant that needs pruning or deadheading. You can use a hand fork and trowel and kneel between each plant and try to dig out every root. Use a waterproof kneeling pad to be more comfortable. Other people prefer hoeing, which removes shallow-rooted annual weeds but this cuts off deep-rooted perennials, which should be dug up. The best hoe for weeding is a Dutch hoe.

If you don't have the time or energy to clear out all the weeds before you plant the first year, try to outcompete them. Rather than sowing seeds straight into the soil, sow them in biodegradeable modules – small pots made of peat or paper – which can be planted straight into the ground. Don't plant perennials the first year or you may have to dig them out later on just to untangle the weeds from their roots, if they survive at all. Instead sow annual flowers and large-seeded plants, such as sunflowers, beans and squash, which need minimal weeding. Even if some of the annuals are drowned out by weed competition, the seeds cost very little and you will have something pretty to show. Don't leave the ground bare, because that gives weeds the chance to get a foothold. Keep the garden mulched to keep weeds in check.

Often the most sensible option for very weedy ground is to smother the weeds before you plant. A year before you want to plant, cover the ground with a mulch to smother the weeds. You can use a biodegradeable mulch, such as cardboard, shredded bark, or sawdust. Or you can buy porous weed control fabric that stops weeds effectively but doesn't stop soil life from working. Heavy-duty black plastic is cheaper to use, but if left in place for more than a few months, it starves the soil creatures as well as the weeds. If you use a fabric covering, lay a layer of bark chips on top to keep it in place and to camouflage the unattractive fabric.

Weed Gallery

When you're growing plants from soil, it's useful to know what weeds actually look like—be careful not to remove the wrong seedlings.

Redroot Pigweed

Common Groundsel

Fleabane

Lamb's Quarters

Shepherd's Purse

BEST TIME TO WEED

Weed when the soil is moist (not wet or it may compact). Weeds are easier to pull from moist soil.

AVOID HERBICIDES

Don't use weedkillers, or herbicides, unless your garden is so overtaken with perennial weeds that you have no hope of taming it. Weedkillers also kill soil life, and many are nonspecific, killing desirable plants as well as weeds. If you do opt to use an herbicide, glyphosate is probably the least damaging, since it breaks down pretty quickly and does not linger for long in the soil.

Common Weeds

Ten annual garden weeds	Ten perennial garden weeds
Amaranthus retrofolia, redroot pigweed	*Cirsium spp.*, Canada thistle
Ambrosia artemisiifolia, ragweed	*Convolvolus arvensis*, bindweed
Capsella bursa-pastoris, shepherd's purse	*Cynodon dactylon*, Bermuda grass
Chenopodium album, lamb's quarters	*Epilobium angustifolium*, northern willowherb
Erigeron annuus, fleabane	*Glechoma hederacea*, ground ivy
Euphorbia maculata, spotted spurge	*Plantago major*, plantain
Euphorbia supina, prostrate spurge	*Ranunculus repens*, creeping buttercup
Poa annuua, annual bluegrass	*Rosa multiflora*, wild rose
Senecio vulgaris, common groundsel	*Rumex spp.*, dock
Stellaria media, chickweed	*Taraxacum officinale*, dandelion

SOIL IN CONTAINERS

Container soil needs to contain plenty of nutrition and to stand up to very regular watering without turning soggy. Ordinary garden soil isn't the best growing medium for containers, because few containers are large enough to build up a living soil complete with all the necessary organisms. Soil for containers also needs to be lighter in weight than garden soil, so air and moisture can pass easily through it, given its smaller volume.

To grow plants in pots make sure you place a few stones or wood chips in the bottom before the soil. This allows for oxygen and drainage.

The great thing about using packaged potting mix is that it is sterilized so you start off free from weed seeds, harmful bacteria, and disease-causing organisms. Most container-grown plants do best in soil-based potting mix, available from most garden centers. It is smart to beef up packaged potting mix with a handful or two (depending on the size of the container) of a slow-release plant food such as chicken-manure pellets (available from online sources), or one or two organic fertilizer spikes. You may also want to add a few handfuls of sand for drainage. If weight is an issue, for example on a roof garden or balcony, add one-third perlite to the potting mix along with your fertilizer. This is an expanded rock product that is lightweight and water absorbent, releasing water slowly as plants need it.

If you're offered a peat-based medium, you may wish to ask for an alternative. Peat is not a resource that is renewable (at least in our lifetime—it takes millennia for peat to form). Alternatives are usually made from coir—a by-product of the coconut industry. Coir absorbs water well and is free-draining like peat, and—unlike peat—quick to reabsorb water if it is allowed to dry out.

Another important consideration for container plants is drainage. To improve drainage in large pots, tubs, and barrels, put a 2-inch (5-cm) layer of pebbles, fine gravel, or filtering charcoal (not barbecue briquettes) in the bottom of the pot. A drainage layer is especially helpful in containers that do not have a drainage hole in the bottom to allow excess water to drain off.

MAKE YOUR OWN POTTING MIX

You can make your own potting mix. Basically what you need are soil, organic matter, and a lightening agent. Here are some recipes. Mix the ingredients well and moisten before planting.

All-purpose mix #1
3 parts potting soil
2 parts crumbled or sieved compost or leaf mold
1 part sharp builder's sand or perlite

All-purpose mix #2
2 parts soil
1 part crumbled or sieved compost
1 part sharp sand or perlite

Rich mix (for humus lovers)
1 part soil
2 parts compost
1 part sharp builder's sand

Growing Potatoes in Containers

If you have a small garden, one space-saving idea is to grow produce in containers. Some people question the wisdom of growing potatoes, because they are relatively inexpensive to buy. Once you taste fresh potatoes from your own garden, however, you'll understand. Also recently harvested potatoes are packed with vitamin C, one benefit you won't get from the stored, frozen, and shipped potatoes in the supermarket.

8 inches
(20 cm)

1 A plastic trash can makes a perfect container to grow potatoes. Drill 8 holes in the base and 8 more around the can about 8 inches (20 cm) up from the bottom for drainage.

12 inches
(30 cm)

2 Pour 12 inches (30 cm) of multipurpose potting mix into the can. Mix it with a spadeful of compost and some well-rotted manure, or a handful of chicken manure pellets.

3 Place two seed potatoes on top and cover them with more compost (use seed potatoes—sprouting spuds from your vegetable basket won't reliably produce a crop.) Water daily except in very rainy weather.

8 inches
(20 cm)

4 When their shoots are about 8 inches (20 cm) above the compost, add another layer of compost to just cover them. Keep doing this until you have reached the top of your container.

5 Harvest the potatoes when their flowers have finished blooming and the tubers are big enough to eat.

ALL ABOUT FLOWERS

Plants are the heart of every garden. You can create fabulous structures, you can have a brilliantly planned outdoor space for playing, relaxing, and entertaining, but it is the plants that bring life into a garden. Some striking gardens rely on the shape, habit, and color of a few specimens, but it can be surprisingly difficult to restrict yourself to a limited selection. Most gardeners start off choosing only a few plants, but as you handle plants more, you'll get increasingly enthusiastic. Before you know it, you will have embarked on a full-blown and lasting love affair.

To begin your garden, you need to understand the current growing conditions. Then you need to consider what kinds of flowers you want to grow—annuals, perennials, or bulbs. Growing heirloom flowers and saving seeds helps preserve the variety of generic material available to plant breeders.

CHOOSING THE RIGHT PLANTS FOR DIFFERENT SITUATIONS

When choosing flowers and other plants, the most important thing is to make sure they suit your garden in terms of your growing conditions and climate. Look through books to help you decide, and make a list of possibilities before you take a trip to the nursery or garden center. Do not consider trying to grow tropical plants in cold, damp, shady gardens, or shade lovers on a sunny bank. Make life easy for you and your plants.

If some gloriously flowering plant seduces you at the garden center, ask someone what conditions the plant needs or check the plant label carefully. A label should tell you whether a plant needs sun or will grow in shade, whether it likes soil that is constantly moist or well-drained, and whether it needs protection from frost or will happily sit outside year-round. The label will also indicate the plant's eventual height and spread, but don't take this as a precise guide, because the size will depend in part on the conditions. Temperature is also important. If a label says, "Tender," this usually means a plant needs temperatures above at least 40°F (5°C).

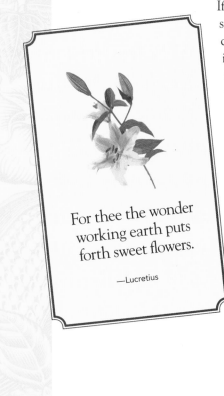

For thee the wonder working earth puts forth sweet flowers.

—Lucretius

If you don't like the look of plant labels stuck around your plants, file them away for reference, but never throw them out.

Light for Your Plants

Most plant labels or gardening books tell you how much light a plant needs. These levels are broken down into four categories: full sun, partial shade, light or dappled shade, and deep shade.

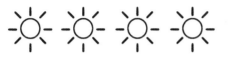

Full sun means that plants are in full sun for most of the day on sunny days. Mediterranean plants, alpines, and desert plants love these conditions, as well as many perennials and annuals.

Partial shade means an area is shaded by trees and shrubs for part of the day on sunny days. A location that is sunny for two to six hours a day is considered to be in partial shade. Many gardens are partially shady and few plants will object.

Light shade describes the dappled shade cast across an area by the shifting light and shadows of leaves and branches of trees. Light shade suits spring bulbs and woodland plants.

Deep shade is usually caused by buildings or dense evergreen hedges or thick trees with large, dense leaves. No direct sun reaches areas in deep shade and only ferns, ivies, and a few woodland plants can cope.

A rule in gardening never forget: sow dry and set wet.

TYPES OF FLOWERING PLANTS

Flowering plants come in many forms, and we define them by their life cycles (annual, biennial, perennial; herbaceous, woody, or bulbous); their tolerance for cold (hardy, half-hardy, tender); their growing habits (ground covering, climbing); and how they are used in gardens (such as bedding plants).

Annuals, Perennials, and Biennials

Here are some definitions of flowering plants. Decide which work best for your garden plan.

Annuals are plants that are around for only one season, during which they germinate, grow, flower, set seed, and die.

Hardy annuals (HA) can tolerate a fair amount of frost and grow best in cool weather. Many hardy annuals can be sown outdoors in fall to sprout the following spring. In warm climates they are grown for winter flowers. Many, such as pansies and cornflowers, may scatter their seed around your garden to produce more plants next year.

That, of al the floures
in the meade,
Thanne love I most thise
floures white and rede,
Swich as men callen
daysyes in our toun.

—Geoffrey Chaucer,
The Canterbury Tales

Half-hardy annuals (HHA) need warmth to germinate and can tolerate cool, damp conditions and a bit of light frost, but can't stand prolonged cold—think cosmos, salvias, and petunias.

Tender annuals (TA) cannot withstand any frost at all and need warm conditions to grow well. Marigolds and zinnias are tender annuals. Some tender perennials that cannot tolerate frost, such as coleus and impatiens, are grown like annuals and discarded after the growing season ends.

Perennial plants, such as asters, astilbe, sedums, and delphiniums are the backbone of most flower gardens. They last for years, happily growing bigger in the ground each year. You may see them called herbaceous perennials, which just means that they don't have a woody stem and usually die down and hide beneath the ground each winter to reappear in spring. Perennials vary in the degree of cold they can tolerate; choose plants for your garden that are hardy in your part of the country.

Biennials have a two-year cycle, typically spending the first year as an insignificant mound of leaves and then blooming, then dying, in their second year. Many biennials seed themselves to produce a new generation of plants so that you don't have to buy new plants after the two years are up. Hollyhocks and foxgloves are biennials.

Bulbous Plants

Bulbous plants are ornamental species that generally rest during winter (though summer-resting bulbous plants do exist) and then grow and flower during spring or summer.

Bulbs are plump underground storage organs from which roots and shoots grow. Daffodils and tulips are the best-known bulbs, but there are dozens of others for spring, summer, and fall flowering.

Then Nature said,
"A lovelier flower
on earth was
never sown."

—William Wordsworth

Corms look like solid bulbs. They are modified underground stems that behave like bulbs.

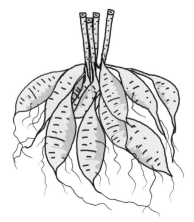

Tubers, such as dahlias, are fleshy underground stems that root and produce shoots.

A CAUTION ABOUT GROUNDCOVER

Be wary of plants labeled as being "good for groundcover." Many of them, such as bishop's weed (*Aegopodium podograria*), will quickly take over an area, often by means of spreading roots.

...there can be no
perfect flower
without fragrance.

—Arthur Symons

HEIRLOOM PLANTS

Heirloom vegetables and flowers are varieties that have been grown in gardens for decades or possibly centuries. They are open-pollinated, which means they are pollinated by bees and other insects rather than any interference from humans. Open-pollinated plants will produce offspring from seed that are just like the parent plants.

Hybrid plants are artificially cross-pollinated and are often bred for specific characteristics, such as longer stems, higher yields, or more uniform shape and size. Many garden flowers and vegetables are hybrids; this means breeders have crossed parent plants with features they like and produced hybrid seed. Plants grown from hybrid seed will not in the future "come true," so gardeners can't save the seed for another year but have to buy new seed each time. Heirloom plants, on the other hand, will come true forever, adapting over time to whatever climate and soil they are grown in. Gardeners can collect and save seeds of heirloom varieties from their gardens.

Many hybrid plants are extremely worthwhile, but their introduction has meant less variety and choice, because breeders focus on developing more and more hybrids with qualities that suit current tastes and the needs of commerce. Vegetables are bred for uniformity and ability to withstand shipping. Where flowers are concerned, some breeders focus on bigger flowers, shorter stems, and brighter colors at the expense of other qualities, such as fragrance. For example, you can find dozens of varieties of pinks and carnations (*Dianthus* spp.) in garden centers, many of them bred to have long stems and large-flowered multicolored heads, but without the glorious spicy-sweet clove fragrance that characterizes old-fashioned heirloom pinks. Heirloom flowers are often more fragrant than modern forms of the same plant.

Heirloom flowers may have different qualities, such as shorter stems or smaller blooms than the type of flower large-scale producers and modern florists want. But heirloom varieties will outproduce many modern plants in areas where they have adapted to climate and soil conditions. Many have greater disease and insect resistance so they are invaluable to organic gardeners.

Heirloom roses are prized for their beautiful full blooms. Gallicas, Damasks, Albas, Centifolias, and Mosses are the five families that make up the heirloom class of roses.

20 Heirloom Flowers to Grow

Annuals	Perennials and Biennials
Gomphrena globosa, globe amaranth	*Agastache foeniculum*, anise hyssop
Helianthus annuus, sunflower	*Alcea rosea*, hollyhock
Heliotropium arborescens, heliotrope	*Aquilegia vulgaris*, columbine
Impatiens balsamina, balsam	*Campanula medium*, Canterbury bells
Lathyrus odoratus, sweet pea	*Chrysanthemum parthenium*, feverfew
Mirabilis jalapa, four o'clock	*Dianthus plumarius*, cottage pink
Nicotiana sylvestris	*Dictamnus albus*, gas plant
Nigella damascena, love-in-a-mist	*Lychnis coronaria*, rose campion
Tagetes 'Lemon Gem', signet marigold	*Platycodon grandiflorus*, balloon flower
Tithonia rotundifolia, Mexican sunflower	*Viola odorata*, sweet violet

Easy Heirloom Varieties

These are some relatively common heirloom varieties that are easy to grow and produce stunning flowers. They have different needs, but don't require anything too extraordinary.

Globe amaranth likes full sun and will bloom in mid-summer.

Heliotrope seedlings need to be planted a few weeks after the last frost of spring.

Sunflowers need careful staking to prevent them falling over as they grow.

Sweet pea should be sown in mid-fall for flowing the following summer.

Four o'clock grows best in full sun. It will die back with the first frost and grow again the spring.

Balsam is fast-growing and will bloom for 60 to 70 days.

Saving Heirlooms

Thanks to their genetics, heirloom plants are often resistant to local pests, diseases, and extreme weather conditions and will gradually adapt to your conditions. They have historical interest and are often extremely beautiful. However, the most important reason for growing the old varieties is that heirloom plants represent a vast and diverse pool of genetic characteristics that will be lost forever if the plants are allowed to become extinct. Even plants that seem somewhat inferior may hold a key to disease resistance or a valuable compound that is vital to future generations of gardeners and plant breeders.

To make sure heirloom plants survive, we can all strive to keep growing and propagating them. Some regional seed companies sell heirloom seeds, and many local garden clubs and plant societies have seed exchanges where you can trade seeds with other members. You can also swap seeds with friends and neighbors or join a larger group such as the Seed Saver's Exchange (www.seedsavers.org).

Every fall you can harvest the seeds that will keep little bits of history alive for one more year. Many of these old varieties would not be around today if it were not for home seed savers.

TESTING SAVED SEED

If you want to determine that your annual seed is good before sowing, germinate some on a sheet of folded damp paper on a small plate. Seed should start to sprout within four to seven days.

Seed pods

When the flowers die back, it's time to harvest your seeds. The seed pods will be easy to locate; here are some basic shapes to look for.

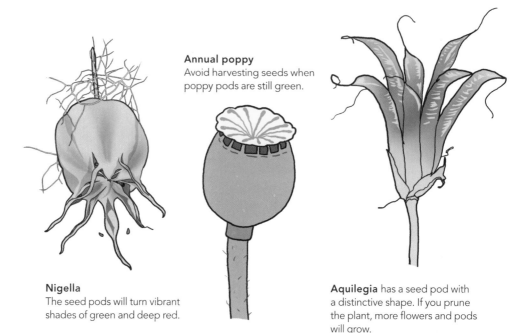

Annual poppy
Avoid harvesting seeds when poppy pods are still green.

Nigella
The seed pods will turn vibrant shades of green and deep red.

Aquilegia has a seed pod with a distinctive shape. If you prune the plant, more flowers and pods will grow.

Saving Seeds

Saving seeds allows you to keep growing the plants you love, efficiently and reliably—often getting better germination and stronger, healthier results than with packaged seeds from the store. There are a few key points to remember to keep varieties pure, but otherwise the process is very easy. Most seed will store for at least two years as long as it stays cool and dry, but sweet pea seed is best sown the year after it is collected because it doesn't remain viable for long.

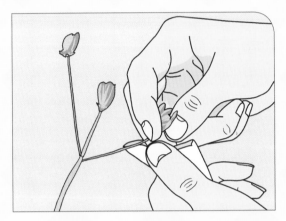

1 When plants have finished flowering, allow their seed heads to ripen and collect them just before the casings split open and seeds fall to the ground. Be sure to collect seeds from dry plants.

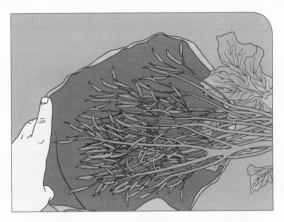

2 If the weather is damp or you are worried you might miss the moment, pull up whole plants just before their seed heads ripen and leave them hanging upside down in an airy place to dry, placing a paper bag over their heads to catch seeds as they drop.

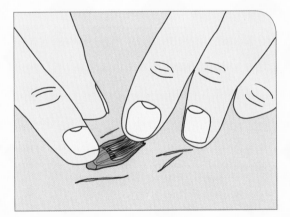

3 You may need to separate seeds from their casings, either by picking through them by hand or shaking them in a flat sieve.

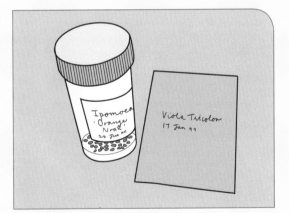

4 Save clean seeds in paper envelopes in a cool, dry place, labeling each packet with the variety and the date. Or save seed in well-labeled screwtop jars in the refrigerator.

HOW AND WHERE TO USE ANNUALS

Annuals provide a great show of color more quickly than any other group of flowering plants. They are wonderful for filling gaps or providing colorful accents in developing perennial borders, and they are showy when planted in blocks of solid or mixed colors. You can find annuals in virtually every flower color and height, many with interesting leaf textures. Most hardy annuals will resow themselves to fill gaps for years to come. These are the ones often preferred, providing plants for free year after year—it's a delight to come across a beautiful clump of poppies that made their own way into your bed or a drift of love-in-a-mist, a scented patch of nicotiana, or a cheerful throng of nasturtiums. Self-seeders are also a great excuse for minimal weeding; if you weed too thoroughly, you won't give them a chance to find themselves new homes.

Many annuals are ideal for containers, roof gardens, terraces, patios and decks, while annual vines, such as morning glories, look wonderful clambering over fences, arbors, and trellises. No country garden is complete without a teepee or two of deliciously scented sweet peas in summer.

Annuals require a bit of work in spring and early summer, when you have to sow them into well-prepared seed beds or pots of compost and keep them well watered and protected from slugs and other bugs, because they are at their vulnerable early stages. Once they are past the seedling stage, they need regular maintenance—watering, feeding, and deadheading. Give your potted annuals some TLC and they will reward you with lavish blooms all summer.

20 Great Annuals for Pots

Ageratum houstonianum, flossflower	*Impatiens* cvs.
Angelonia angustifolia, summer snapdragon	*Lantana* cvs.
Argyranthemum frutescens, marguerite daisy	*Lobelia erinus*, edging lobelia
Calendula officinalis, pot marigold	*Lobularia maritima*, sweet alyssum
Calibrachoa cvs., million bells	*Pelargonium* spp., geraniums
Catharanthus roseus, Madagascar periwinkle	*Petunia integrifolia*
Cosmos spp.	*Salvia farinacea* 'Victoria' or 'Blue Bedder'
Cuphea hyssopifolia, Mexican heather	*Tagetes* spp., marigold
Fuchsia x *hybrida*	*Tropaeolum majus*, nasturtium
Heliotropium arborescens, heliotrope	*Verbena* x *hybrida* cvs., garden verbena

CUTTING GARDENS

One of the great joys of summer is filling vases with freshly cut flowers, especially when you've grown them yourself. Many annuals and perennials make good cut flowers, and annuals are especially welcome, because they provide flowers for most or all of the summer. For the greatest selection, put your cutting garden in a sunny spot. See below for some suggestions to get your cutting garden started.

20 Great Cutting Flowers

Antirrhinum majus, snapdragon	*Gypsophila paniculata*, baby's breath
Aster spp.	*Helianthus* spp., sunflower
Calendula officinalis, pot marigold	*Iris sibirica*
Callistephus chinensis, China aster	*Lathyrus odoratus*, sweet pea
Centaura cyanus, bachelor's button, cornflower	*Leucanthemum* x *superbum*, Shasta daisy
Cerinthe major 'Purpurascens', honeywort	*Lilium* spp., lilies
Cleome hassleriana, spider flower	*Nigella damascena*, love-in-a-mist
Consolida ambigua, larkspur	*Papaver* spp., poppy
Cosmos spp.	*Rudbeckia* spp., black-eyed Susan
Dianthus barbatus, sweet William	*Salvia* spp., sage

Cauterizing Flowers

Some flowers ooze a sticky substance when cut, and then this dries, preventing them absorbing any water. These flowers need to be cauterized to make them last. Place them in 2 inches (5 cm) of just boiled water for 30 seconds, then plunge into cool water and leave for at least an hour.

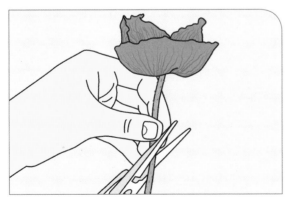

1 Poppies, hydrangeas, hollyhocks, and daffodils are all flowers that ooze a sticky substance, sealing the end of the stem. For these flowers, determine the appropriate stem height, and trim with scissors.

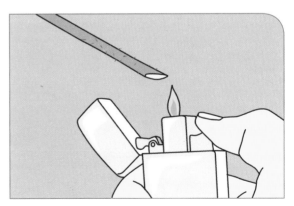

2 Singe the cut ends briefly with a flame. A handheld lighter works well for this. Arrange as usual in water, and your flowers will last weeks instead of days.

BEDDING PLANTS AND BEDDING SCHEMES

Some showy plants are known as bedding plants, which are used in closely planted masses for a seasonal display to fill specific beds or areas in your garden with a mass of color. Most bedding plants are annual or tender plants, but pansies and tulips are also popular for winter (in warm climates) and spring bedding schemes.

You need a greenhouse or polytunnel if you want to grow your own bedding plants (see Chapter 7, pages 144–171); it is much easier to buy them locally in early summer. You may find them at yard sales or farmers' markets, often much cheaper than at garden centers.

Before you go shopping, think about your color schemes and plant combinations. Do you want to create patches of vibrant color? Cover a bed in a pattern? If you opt for brilliant colors, such as reds, oranges, and bright yellows together, you may want to include some white in the mix to tone down the colors and keep them from clashing. White flowers and silver foliage can also allow contrasting colors to blend visually.

Bedding plants can be arranged in decorative and intricate shapes. Most are annuals, so you can try different designs each year.

Summer Bedding

Set out summer bedding plants when all danger of frost has passed, and the soil has warmed. Prepare the ground well by weeding thoroughly and raking in compost before planting in large drifts or clumps. Or follow a specific pattern you have marked out on the ground with sand. Beds of annuals only last for one season, so you can replant and get a fresh start next spring, giving your garden a completely new identity each year.

A VICTORIAN CARPET BED

In the nineteenth century in England, gardeners planted elaborate carpet beds with low plants laid out in detailed patterns, sometimes inspired by the designs of oriental carpets. To create your own Victorian carpet bed, sketch the design on paper and plan the color scheme. When you are ready to plant, mark the pattern on the bed with lime, sand, or landscape marking paint. Start small—you can always make a bigger bed next year.

For a simple pattern for your first carpet bed, try dividing a square or rectangular bed into quarters, with two diagonal lines running across the bed from corner to corner. Plant one type and color of flower in two of the sections and a different color in the other two. Make a border all around the outer edge of the bed in a third color.

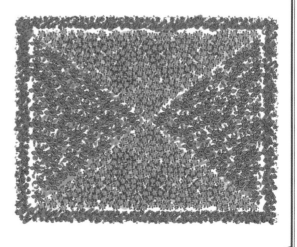

Winter Bedding

Winter bedding is possible in mild regions. If you are lucky enough to be able to grow flowers in winter, locate the beds where you can see them from your windows or pass them often as you come and go from your house. It is lovely to fill a small bed with bright winter bedding or plant in windowboxes or containers. Winter-flowering pansies, fragrant stocks, ivies, and heathers are good candidates. For early spring, consider cyclamen and primroses. Let spring burst forth with tulips, daffodils, narcissus, and hyacinths planted in larger or more distant beds and viewed from the garden as well as glimpsed from the windows of your house.

CARE FOR BEDDING PLANTS

For the best show, water your bedding plants well each evening and keep them well weeded, and feed every couple of weeks with compost tea or another all-purpose liquid fertilizer.

HAVE SUMMER IN WINTER

In late summer or early fall, take cuttings from annual flowers, such as impatiens, geraniums, and wax begonias, and root them in pots for winter flowers indoors. Cut the tip of a healthy stem 4–6 inches (10–15 cm) long, cutting on a slant, just above the second set of leaves from the top. Remove any flowers or buds, and place the bottom of the cutting in a pot of moist potting mix. Enclose the planted cutting and pot in a clear plastic bag, holding the bag off the cutting with Popsicle sticks or short, slender stakes. Keep the pot out of direct sun. Water as needed to keep the soil evenly moist but not soggy. When roots have formed—a gentle tug on the plant will meet with resistance—remove the plastic and move the pot to a sunny windowsill.

A Dozen Summer Bedding Plants

Ageratum houstonianum, flossflower—blue, lavender, or white flowers between June and September. 9–12 inches (25–30 cm) high.

Antirrhinum majus, snapdragon—vertical spikes of pink, red, yellow, or white flowers between June and September. 9–24 inches (25–60 cm); use smaller varieties for bedding.

Begonia semperflorens, wax begonia—flowers between June and October. Red, white, and pink rose-type flowers in profusion. 6–9 inches (15–25 cm).

Gomphrena globosa, globe amaranth—ball-shaped flowerheads of magenta, purple, pink, white, or red on branched plants. 6–24 inches (15–60 cm).

Impatiens cvs., bedding impatiens—blooms all summer until frost in shades of red, pink, rose, lavender, orange, white. 8–12 inches (20–30 cm).

Lobelia erinus, edging lobelia—masses of small blue, red, white, or mauve flowers between June and October. 6 inches (15 cm).

Lobularia maritima, sweet alyssum—small plants with clusters of tiny white or purple honey-scented flowers from early spring to fall. 3–10 inches (8–25 cm). Cut back to encourage rebloom in summer.

Pelargonium spp., geranium—a huge range of bedding geraniums in red, white, salmon, rose, and pink make a show all summer as long as you keep deadheading. 12–18 inches (30–45 cm).

Petunia x *hybrida*, petunia—profusely flowering all summer long in singles and doubles, shades of pinks, purples, red, blue, yellow, and white. 9–12 inches (25–30 cm).

Phlox drummondii, annual phlox—clusters of late spring and summer flowers in shades of purple, pink, red, and white. 6–18 inches (15–45 cm).

Salvia splendens, scarlet sage—dark green leaves and bright scarlet, violet, salmon, purple, or white flowers from June to frost. 9–12 inches (25–30 cm).

Tagetes spp., marigold—flowers all summer, oranges, yellows, and mahogany red. 6–12 inches (15–30 cm).

PERENNIALS AND BIENNIALS

Perennials bloom year after year, and you can choose from thousands of plants in a huge variety of colors, shapes, and sizes. Most are easy to work with, needing only enough light, good soil, and sufficient water to reward you with a mass of flowers. Biennials are also valuable in the garden; each plant will only flower for one year but many biennials will self-sow to produce another generation. Within a few years your garden can be full of biennials, such as hollyhocks, honesty, evening primrose, and foxgloves.

Since perennials remain in the ground for years, give the plants the conditions they like at the start, especially the right levels of sun or shade. In a sunny garden you can grow sun lovers. For a shady spot plant shade-tolerant plants. Keep the soil in good condition by continuing to add compost and other organic matter and feeding plants annually with natural fertilizers. Try to weed around perennials and biennials regularly so they don't get weeds tangling up in their roots and competing for resources. You will also need to deadhead to remove faded flowers, divide the plants to keep them vigorous, and prune or cut them back when necessary. You will find information on caring for plants in Caring for Your Garden on pages 142–171.

BEDS AND BORDERS

Perennials are best displayed in beds and borders. Whether you want to have a classic herbaceous border or a small bed tucked in near the front door, you can fill it with color. A well-planned border can be interesting from spring to fall, with continuous seasonal flowers and foliage. It takes experience to create the perfect perennial border, working out contrasting and complementary heights, colors, textures, and flowering times, but it's fun getting that experience.

Shed no tear!
O shed no tear!
The flower will bloom
another year.

—John Keats

20 Sun-Loving Perennials	
Achillea spp., yarrow	*Kniphofia uvaria*, red-hot poker
Aster spp.	*Lavandula* spp., lavender
Campanula spp., bellflower	*Leucanthemum* x *superbum*, Shasta daisy
Coreopsis spp., tickseed	*Nepeta* x *faassenii*, catmint
Delphinium spp.	*Paeonia* spp., peony
Gaillardia spp., blanketflower	*Phlox paniculata*, summer phlox
Helenium autumnale, sneezeweed	*Rudbeckia* spp., black-eyed Susan
Helianthus spp., sunflower	*Salvia* spp., sage
Hemerocallis spp., daylily	*Thalictrum* spp., meadowrue
Iris spp.	*Yucca* spp.

Border Basics

The traditional way to plant beds and borders is to put the tallest plants at the back of the garden graduating down in size, with the shortest plants in the front. A gradation of heights adds a feeling of depth to the garden and allows all the flowers to be visible. However, a few tall plants at the front makes a design more interesting and dynamic.

To get the most visual impact from your colors, group the flowers into clumps or drifts; don't just set out one of this or two of that. If you want to have color in a perennial garden throughout the growing season, you will want to plant some flowers that bloom in spring, some for summer, and others to bloom in late summer and fall. Most perennials bloom for three or four weeks, but some flower far longer, and these are especially valuable in the garden.

Perennials are very accommodating plants. As long as you water them well, they can be moved during the growing season whenever the weather is not too stressful. Avoid transplanting during very hot, dry weather. If you are transplanting in summer, make sure to keep the plants well watered for several weeks after you move them and they settle into their new home. You might also give them some shade while they adjust. Deadhead these plants regularly, they may bloom on and on.

KEEPING IN SCALE

When creating a border, keep it in proportion to your property—the bigger the yard, the bigger the border or bed should be. The deeper it is, the more impressive it will look.

PERENNIAL STYLES

Your perennial garden can be in any style you like, and it doesn't have to contain only perennials. It can be very effective to mix shrubs, perennials, and herbs together in beds and borders. You can use them in formal schemes bordered by clipped hedges or surrounding topiary, planting in huge single blocks of color or in more gentle drifts. Or you might prefer a

PLANT ODD NUMBERS

To create a more natural look, plant odd-numbered groups of the same type of plant rather than single specimens or even numbers.

20 Long-Blooming Perennials

Achillea spp., yarrow	*Nepeta* x *fassenii*, catmint
Agrostemma githago 'Milas'	*Nipponanthemum nipponicum*, Montauk daisy
Ceratostigma plumbaginoides, plumbago	*Papaver nudicaule P.*, Summer Breeze Series
Coreopsis spp., tickseed	*Perovskia atriplicifolia*, Russian sage
Dicentra eximia, fringed bleeding heart	*Physostegia virginiana*, obedient plant
Echinacea purpurea, purple coneflower	*Rudbeckia* spp., black-eyed Susan
Gaillardia spp., blanketflower	*Salvia* 'May Night'
Geranium spp., cranesbill (especially *G. sanguineum* var. *striatum*, Lancaster geranium)	*Sedum* 'Autumn Joy', stonecrop
Hemerocallis 'Stella de Oro' and 'Happy Returns', daylily	*Stokesia laevis*, Stokes' aster
Leucanthemum x *superbum*, Shasta daisy	*Veronica* 'Sunny Border Blue' and 'Goodness Grows'

The summer's flower is to the summer sweet, Though to itself it only live and die.

—William Shakespeare

TROUBLESHOOTING PEONIES

If your peonies don't bloom, they may be planted too deeply. Carefully dig up the plants that don't bloom and replant them so the red growth buds on the crown (where the stems meet the roots) are 1–1 ½ inches (2–3 cm) below the soil surface. Handle the plants very carefully as you move them.

more relaxed, informal garden in a rainbow of different colors, where drifts of plants flow together and mix along the edges. You can combine plants in whatever way you like, perhaps starting with some of your favorite flowers. But certain plants have been grown together for centuries, such as delphiniums with peonies or lady's mantle (*Alchemilla mollis*) with catmint (*Nepeta x faassenii*), so you can't go wrong if you use traditional favorites as a starting point, with a few scented roses and clematis climbing up obelisks or wooden frames if you're going for a country look.

An especially charming way to grow plants is in a traditional cottage garden. Cottage gardens are devoted to old-fashioned flowers, and they are all about the plants, rather than a planned-out design. This is the place for your favorite fragrant flowers, and the cuttings and pass-along plants given to you by your grandmother, or gardening friends and neighbors. Cottage gardens are usually fairly small, and many gardeners like to enclose them with a white picket fence.

Minimize the Workload

Although the mixed planting of a traditional border should look relaxed and can even seem haphazard, some perennial borders do take some work. Tall plants may need to be staked, others need to be cut back as soon as they have flowered, and still others need almost daily deadheading in season. If this seems like too much work for you, choose low maintenance plants that require less work to maintain. You could mix the flowering plants with perennial grasses for added interest. Including flowering shrubs in the garden is another way to gain color and form with less work.

Cottage Garden Favorites

Achillea spp., yarrow	*Echinacea purpurea*, purple coneflower	*Paeonia* spp., peony
Aconitum spp., monkshood		*Papaver orientale*, oriental poppy
Alcea spp., hollyhock	*Eryngium* spp., sea holly	
Aster spp.	*Geranium* spp., cranesbill	*Penstemon* spp., beard-tongue
Astrantia major, masterwort	*Helenium autumnale*, sneezeweed	*Phlox paniculata*, summer phlox
Campanula spp., bellflower	*Kniphofia uvaria*, red-hot poker	*Rosa* cvs., roses
Crocosmia 'Lucifer', montbretia	*Lavandula* spp., lavender	*Rudbeckia* spp., black-eyed Susan
Delphinium spp.	*Lobelia siphilitica*, great blue lobelia	*Salvia* spp., sage
Dianthus gratianopolitanus, cheddar pink	*Lunaria annuua*, honesty	*Stachys byzantina*, lamb's ears
	Monarda didyma, beebalm	*Verbena bonariensis*, vervain

20 Great Low-Maintenance Perennials

Acanthus spinosus, spiny bear's breeches	*Iris sibirica*, Siberian iris
Achillea 'Coronation Gold', yarrow	*Perovskia atriplicifolia*, Russian sage
Asclepias tuberosa, butterfly weed	*Phlox divaricata*, wild blue phlox
Astrantia major, masterwort	*Platycodon grandiflorus*, balloon flower
Brunnera macrophylla, Siberian bugloss	*Pulmonaria* spp., Bethlehem sage
Cimicifuga racemosa, snakeroot	*Rudbeckia* spp., black-eyed Susan
Crocosmia 'Lucifer', montbretia	*Sedum* spp., stonecrop
Filipendula spp., meadowsweet	*Solidago* spp., goldenrod
Gaura lindheimeri	*Stachys byzantina*, lamb's ear
Helianthemum nummularium, sunrose	*Veronicastrum virginicum*, Culver's root

ORNAMENTAL GRASSES

Ornamental grasses work beautifully with perennials in informal gardens, where they add texture and graceful movement as they sway in the breeze. They're easy to care for—just cut them back once a year, in late fall or winter.

Calamagrostis x acutiflora 'Karl Foerster', feather reed grass (medium height)

Carex spp., sedges (short to medium height)

Chasmanthium latifolium, northern sea oats (medium)

Elymus arenarius 'Glaucus', blue lyme grass (medium)

Festuca glauca, blue fescue grass (short)

Hakonechloa macra 'Aureola', hakone grass (short, for shade)

Miscanthus sinensis, many varieties, eulalia grass (tall)

Molinia caerulea, purple moor grass (medium)

Panicum virgatum, switchgrass (tall)

Pennisetum alopecuroides 'Moudry', black-flowered fountain grass (medium)

Stipa gigantea, golden oats (tall)

Rub the inside of a beehive with the flowers of thyme, fennel, and hyssop so the bees will always want to come back to it.

Perennials for Attracting Butterflies and Bees

Butterflies are delightful in the garden, and bees are essential for pollination. Here are some perennials to grow if you want to attract bees and butterflies.

Agastache spp., anise hyssop	*Lupinus* spp., lupine
Asclepias tuberosa, butterfly weed	*Monarda* spp., bergamot
Aster spp.	*Nepeta* x *faassenii*, catmint
Coreopsis spp., tickseed	*Penstemon* spp., beardtongue
Echinacea purpurea, purple coneflower	*Phlox paniculata*, summer phlox
Echinops spp., globe thistle	*Rudbeckia* spp., black-eyed Susan
Eupatorium purpureum, Joe-pye weed	*Salvia coccinea*, Texas sage
Lantana camara (perennial in warm climates)	*Solidago* spp., goldenrod
Liatris spp., gayfeather	*Veronica* spp., speedwell

DON'T CLEAN UP TOO MUCH

Resist the impulse to tidy up the perennial garden too much in fall. Instead leave some seed heads and plant stems standing when the plants die back. The dead plants will not only provide interesting shapes in your garden through the winter but also food and homes for overwintering wildlife.

Foliage Is Important

Most perennials bloom for just a few weeks so, when planning a flower garden, try to include an interesting mix of foliage shapes and textures along with the flowers. Leaves can be rounded, oblong, or narrow; big and bold or delicately incised; spiky or feathery, toothed or scalloped, or smooth along the edges. Some leaves are golden or bluish or silver-gray, others are striped, spotted, flushed, splashed, or marbled with white, gold, pink, red, or purple. In a small garden where there's not enough room to orchestrate a multiseason succession of bloom, foliage can be the star of the show, perhaps mixed with evergreen shrubs and just a few flowers for emphasis. Mix grays, such as lamb's ears and artemisia, with rich greens, such as euphorbias or bergenia, and combine different-shaped leaves, such as linear Solomon's seal, ruffled heucheras, and frilly Japanese painted fern, with soft-textured hostas. Spreading purple and variegated sages look stunning on their own or draping through other foliage.

Perennials for Foliage

The following perennials will still look good, even when not in flower.

Artemisia spp., wormwood	*Persicaria virginiana* 'Painter's Palette', bistort
Athyrium goeringianum 'Pictum', Japanese painted fern, and other ferns	*Pulmonaria* spp., Bethlehem sage, lungwort
Euphorbia spp., spurge	*Salvia officinalis* 'Tricolor' and 'Icterina', sage
Grasses	*Santolina chamaecyparissus*, lavender cotton
Heuchera spp., alumroot	*Stachys byzantina*, lamb's ears
Hosta, many species and varieties	*Tiarella cordifolia*, foamflower
Lamium spp., deadnettle	*Yucca* spp.

BULBOUS PLANTS

Some plants have swollen stems that act as food storage organs, enabling the plants to survive when dormant. These swollen stems may be known as "bulbs," "corms," "tubers," or "rhizomes." For ease of use, the general term "bulb" is used here to describe the whole group.

Spring bulbs do much to lift the spirits, heralding brighter days ahead. And they take up hardly any space; even if your garden is little more than a windowbox you can have spring bulbs and follow them with something else in the same space. They are happy in most situations, except in the deepest shade of conifers.

Snowdrops, crocus, anemones, and many early daffodils look particularly fine under deciduous trees or shrubs, in areas that become too shady to host flowers later in the year but provide dappled shade in spring before leaves form a canopy above. Hyacinths and grape hyacinths are stunning in clumps in your flowerbeds, while *Iris reticulata* needs to be somewhere obvious where its tiny, bright blue-purple flowers can be noticed. Tulips are among the most versatile of bulbs, glorious in clumps and drifts in borders, stunning in containers and brilliant in vases, with hundreds of colors and flower shapes to choose from, and varieties that flower from early spring nearly to summer. Plant lots of the same variety packed closely together to make a big show.

Spring-flowering bulbs should be planted in fall, although snowdrops are best planted "in the green," which means just after they have flowered—before their green stems and stalks die back. As a general rule, plant bulbs two to three times as deep as the height of the bulb and around two bulb widths apart. Plant into soft, crumbly soil, if possible, to stop them becoming waterlogged, but if the ground is particularly rough just do what you can; bulbs will try to grow, whatever the soil conditions. For a natural look, throw daffodil bulbs and crocus corms up in the air and plant them exactly where they land.

BULB PLANTING

Common spring bulbs include snowdrops, tulips, narcissi, daffodils, hyacinths, scilla, grape hyacinths, and fritillaria, along with *Iris reticulata*, (a rhizome), and crocus and *Anemone nemorosa* (both corms).

If deer are a problem in your garden, don't plant tulips—deer love them. Plant daffodils and narcissus instead.

CHOOSE HEALTHY BULBS

When buying bulbs, make sure they are healthy and as fresh as possible. They should be firm, with no soft or moldy patches.

And flowers
through the grass
Joyously sprang
While all the tribes
of birds sang.

—Walter von der Vogelweide

Summer and Fall Bulbs

Summer-flowering bulbs are often overlooked, but they're a wonderful way to add extra variety to a border without using up much space—a bulb is a tiny thing compared to a large rootball. Even if your beds are already fairly full, there's usually room to squeeze in a few alliums or dramatic foxtail lilies (*Eremurus* spp.); bearded iris and true lilies (*Lillium* spp.) are other garden classics and come in a host of colors; many are fragrant, too.

Summer bulbs should be planted in spring, just when the soil is starting to warm up.

CHECKLIST FOR CHOOSING SUMMER BULBS

Hardy Bulbs for Borders Allium, Camassia, Crocosmia, *Eremurus* (foxtail lily), Ixia, Madonna lilies, Regal lilies, Tiger lilies, Turkscap lilies

Bulbs for Moist Sites Calla (Arum) lilies, *Cardiocrinum giganteum* (for warm climates)

Tender Bulbs Agapanthus, Caladium (great for shade), Canna, Dahlias, Eucomis, Gladiolus, Ginger, Watsonia

Best for Containers Agapanthus, Dahlia, many lilies

Glorious Lilies

Some of these flowers are true lilies and some resemble lilies, but all of them are lovely additions to the garden.

Canna cvs., canna—tender, brightly colored, and tropical-looking. In northern climates, grow in containers and bring indoors over winter or grow as annuals; 3–6 feet (90–180 cm).

Cardiocrinum giganteum, giant Himalayan lily—fragrant white trumpet flowers; can grow 12 feet (5 m) tall.

Eremurus spp., foxtail lily—stately plants up to 10 feet (3 m) tall, with large flower spikes of white, yellow, pink, or orange, shaped like foxes' tails.

Lilium candidum, Madonna lily—glistening white, fragrant trumpets; 3–4 feet (90–120 cm) tall.

Lilium lancifolium, tiger lily—orange-red flowers with recurved (backswept) petals; to 5 feet (150 cm).

Lilium regale, regal lily—a classic lily, purply pink outside and white inside, that's easy to grow in most gardens, with a heady perfume; 3–5 feet (90–150 cm).

Lilium superbum, Turkscap lily—orange flowers with recurved (backswept) petals with maroon spots; late blooming; to 10 feet (3 m) tall.

Zantedeschia spp., calla lily—white spathe flowers slowly unfurl inside shiny deep green or mottled foliage; for wet sites; 18 inches (45 cm).

CLIMBING PLANTS

Climbers are a very important group of plants with many roles to play in the landscape. They add vertical line to the garden, take up little ground space, and are especially useful in small spaces and enclosed urban gardens. Climbing plants can direct the eye to a feature or focal point, camouflage an old stump or an ugly chain-link fence, provide screening for privacy, or create shade when trained over an arbor. They can offer flowers, some wonderfully fragrant. They range from useful unshowy ivies and lovely clematis to glorious climbing and rambler roses and huge scented wisterias. There are vines for spring, summer, and fall color as well as decorative winter berries.

Many climbers are vigorous growers and need plenty of moisture and nutrients. It's important to prepare your soil well, especially when planting next to a wall where rain can't easily penetrate. You also need to prepare most walls with wire or trellis supports, even if the climbers are self-supporting, because vigorous climbing vines can damage the surface of buildings. Make the planting hole 12 inches (30 cm) away from the wall and angle the plant back toward the wall. Dig as much organic matter as possible into the hole and supplement this organic matter with a generous feed of an all-purpose fertilizer, then continue to feed regularly as the plant grows.

Types of Climbers

Climbers usually require pruning annually to improve their flowering. Early-flowering plants (blooming before July on new growth) are usually pruned immediately after flowering, and later flowering plants (that bloom on stems formed the previous season) are pruned in early spring.

Clingers Plants in this group naturally attach themselves to a wall and need little, if any, training. Simply point them in the direction of the wall and they will do the rest. Be wary of planting them directly against your house, because they may eventually weaken mortar and damage the surface of old brick and stone. English ivy (*Hedera* spp.), Virginia creeper (*Parthenocissus quinquefolia*), and climbing hydrangea (*Hydrangea petiolaris*) are good examples. Clinging vines may need cutting back if they're growing on a wall and invade a window space. You can do this with shears at any time of the year, but it is probably best to do it in the spring.

CHOOSE GOOD CLIMBERS

When buying climbers, check that there is growth at the base of the plant rather than at the top. It is much better to have a vine with short, strong shoots than one with long bare stems with shoots at the top.

PLANTING CLEMATIS

Clematis needs to be planted 3–4 inches (10–15 cm) deeper than it was in the seller's container. This helps combat clematis wilt, the one disease that affects clematis. Also, according to tradition, clematis grows best in a location where its roots are in the shade and the top of the plant is in the sun.

Twiners and Tendriled Climbers The plants in this group need to be supported on a trellis, netting, or training wires. You may need to tie their shoots to the framework when you first plant them, but once the plants get growing, they will attach themselves. Honeysuckle and wisteria will twist their stems around the support. Clematis pulls itself up by twining its leaf stalks around the support to hold the stems away from it. Passionflower and jasmine have tendrils that twine around the support. Sweet peas need help at the start until they are tall enough to wrap their tendrils around their support.

Scandent (Climbing) Plants These plants do not really climb on their own but can be trained to grow upward on supports. Roses, cotoneaster, and pyracantha need to be fastened to their supports on a regular basis, because they cannot attach themselves.

Roses can be trained to grow on supports. Hide the bare legs of the supports with hardy geraniums or potted plants.

Pyracantha needs to be planted at least 20 inches (50 cm) out from the wall to prevent it from drying out.

Climbing Classics

Climbing roses and clematis are queens among climbers. Give them a location where their tops get plenty of sun, feed them well, and prune them when they need it, and they will reward you with lavish bloom.

Cut back the tips of the stems of climbing and rambler roses by 6 inches (15 cm) when plants finish blooming. In fall or early spring, prune to remove dead and damaged canes. On older plants, cut one or two of the oldest stems back to the ground to encourage new, vigorous growth.

You have to know your type of clematis to know when to prune it. Prune early-blooming species when they finish flowering. Prune summer bloomers in spring.

Prune hybrids in the Florida Group and Patens Group when they finish blooming.

Prune Jackmanii hybrids in winter or early spring, cutting the stems back hard; you can cut them almost to the ground.

Train for Better Blooms

To get more flowers on climbing and rambler roses, train the stems as horizontally as you can, fastening them to supports. This will encourage more lateral stems, which produce the flowers. You will also encourage flowering lower down the plant. Attach stems to the trellis using loosely tied green string or stretchy wire.

Tie shoots to their supports when they are young and supple. However, don't tie too tightly or you may bruise or damage them.

Climbing and Rambler Roses to Grow

Climbing roses	Rambler roses
America, coral-pink, fragrant	American Pillar, pink blend
Cecile Brunner, pale pink, highly scented	Bobby James, creamy white, fragrant
Dortmund, red, single	Crimson Shower, crimson
Etoile de Hollande, deep crimson, scented	Dorothy Perkins, light rose-pink
Gloire de Dijon, buff-colored, fragrant	Paul's Himalayan Musk, pale pink, fragrant
Golden Showers, yellow, fragrant	*Rosa banksiae* 'Lutea', for southern gardens, yellow, double, scented, early-blooming
Madame Gregoire Staechlin, large pink flowers, vigorous climber	Wedding Day, white, single, fragrant
New Dawn, blush pink, fragrant	
William Baffin, deep pink semidouble, very hardy	

Some Clematis Varieties to Grow

Ascotiensis, blue-violet

Comtesse de Bouchard, mauve-pink

Empress, pink double flowers

Ernest Markham, magenta-pink

Etoile Violette, deep purple

Jackmanii, deep purple

Nelly Moser, pink with deep pink stripe on petals

Clematis is separated into roughly 300 known species and is popular worldwide.

TREES AND SHRUBS

If you are planning a new landscape, start with trees and shrubs. These woody plants create the basic structure of the landscape; they are in place year-round and will be there for years. Along with fences, walls, and other structural elements, they anchor and define your outdoor space, so choose them carefully and plan their placement thoughtfully. Some gardens have no flowers and rely entirely on trees and shrubs.

There are two types; deciduous, which lose their leaves in the fall; and evergreen, which retain their leaves, bringing a splash of green to the garden in the depths of winter. They may also offer colored foliage, flowers, fruit (edible or ornamental), and interesting bark.

Although most trees will require less maintenance than the rest of your garden, it's not always the case. Fruit trees may need the occasional spray of insecticide, and most trees and shrubs require some pruning. Think about what you want from your garden. If you're planning a space that's mostly flowers, consider a fruit or a nut tree. Alternatively, if you're devoting large areas to a vegetable patch, you might want to consider more ornamental trees and shrubs. For real impact, hydrangeas, propagated by softwood cuttings, are shrub climbers that can reach up to 10 feet (3 m) tall.

WORKING WITH TREES AND SHRUBS

Trees and shrubs are all woody plants that remain in the garden year after year. Unlike herbaceous perennials, they do not die back to the ground in winter. It can be confusing to figure out the difference between a shrub and a tree, since some trees are multistemmed like shrubs, and some shrubs are as large as small trees. Generally speaking, trees have a main trunk and a definite crown. Shrubs are often bushier, without a central crown, and have branches closer to the ground. Deciduous trees and shrubs lose their leaves in winter, while evergreens keep them on all winter.

If trees and shrubs are already in place on your property, try to incorporate them into your plans, if they are healthy. If you are planting new ones, opt for native species when possible; they are adapted to the regional climate and growing conditions and will be likely to thrive with a minimum of care.

ATTRIBUTES OF TREES AND SHRUBS

Trees and shrubs bring a lot to the garden. They offer shade, flowers, ornamental or edible fruit, and color in summer or fall or, in the case of evergreens, all year long. Some have decorative bark. They supply food and homes for the wildlife that is so important to our gardens—small insects and flying creatures, squirrels, and toads and, of course, birds. You can use trees and shrubs as individual focal points or as hedges and screens for privacy, windbreak, marking boundaries, or defining spaces. Shrubs and small trees work beautifully in mixed borders with perennials, bulbs, annuals, and ornamental grasses.

Choose trees and shrubs with an informal habit for a natural look, and let them grow to their natural shapes. In a formal garden, rely on evergreens that respond well to shaping and shearing (and keep them carefully clipped) or that have a naturally neat growth habit.

Easy-Care Trees and Shrubs

For low-maintenance, woody plants, try these:

Trees River birch (*Betula nigra*), Hornbeam (*Carpinus* spp.), Saucer magnolia (*Magnolia soulangeana*), Serviceberry (*Amelanchier* spp.), Japanese zelkova (*Zelkova serrata*).

Shrubs Bayberry (*Myrica pensylvanica*), Holly (*Ilex* spp.), Forsythia (*Forsythia* spp.) Juniper (*Juniperus* spp.), Spirea (*Spiraea* spp.), Viburnum (*Viburnum* spp.), Witch hazel (*Hamamelis* spp.).

Shrubs and Small Trees for Mixed Borders and Small Gardens

Acer palmatum var. *dissectum*, dwarf Japanese maple cultivars	*Kolkwitzia amabilis*, beautybush
	Lonicera x *purpussi*, 'Winter Beauty'
Aucuba japonica, gold dust plant	*Magnolia* spp.
Buddleia spp., butterfly bush	*Mahonia aquifolium*, Oregon grape holly
Buxus spp., boxwood	*Philadelphus* spp., mock orange
Callicarpa spp., beautyberry	*Prunus* spp., flowering cherry
Camellia spp.	*Rhododendron* spp., azalea and rhododendron
Ceanothus spp., California lilac	
Cornus spp., dogwood	*Salix gracilistyla*, roseglow pussy willow
Hamamelis spp., witch hazel	*Spiraea* spp., spirea
Hydrangea spp.	*Styrax* spp., snowbell
Ilex spp., hollies	*Viburnum* spp.
Kerria japonica, Japanese kerria	*Weigela florida*

You don't have to stick with evergreens for interest in winter; there are trees with interesting bark and deciduous shrubs with colored stems or colorful berries. But do plant one or two evergreens, such as a shiny-leaved camellia or a pair of hollies (you need both male and female plants if you want the bright berries) as good background structure. Golden varieties of evergreens bring a glow to the gray winter landscape. Warm-climate gardeners can enjoy winter-blooming camellias, honeysuckle, and other shrubs. Silver-gray foliage also looks stunning in winter; one of the most dramatic is shrubby germander (*Teucrium fruticans*), a warm-climate plant that boasts slender silver stems and an elegant spreading habit.

Golden Evergreens

Cedrus deodara 'Aurea Pendula', golden weeping deodar	*Juniperus communis* 'Gold Cone'
	Pinus strobus 'Hillside Winter Gold', golden white pine
Cephalotaxus harringtonia 'Korean Gold', golden plum yew	*Pinus sylvestris* 'Aurea' and 'Gold Coin', golden Scots pine
Chamaecyparis lawsoniana 'Golden Showers', golden lawson cypress	*Pinus virginiana* 'Wate's Golden'
	Sequoia sempervirens 'Silba's Golden'
Chamaecyparis nootkanensis 'Aurea' and 'Aureovarie gata', yellow Alaska cedar	*Taxus cuspidata* 'Bright Gold', golden Japanese yew
Chamecyparis pisifera 'Lemon Thread'	*Thuja occidentalis* 'Golden Globe', 'Sunkist', and 'Yellow Ribbon', golden arborvitae
Cryptomeria japonica 'Barabit's Gold'	
Cupressus macrocarpa 'Golden Pillar', golden Monterey cypress	*Thuja orientalis* 'Aurea Nana'
Juniperus chinensis 'Pfitzeriana Aurea'	*Thuja plicata* 'Collyer's Gold'

TREES

Planting trees is a noble occupation for gardeners. In addition to the many benefits they bring to our gardens, trees are good for the planet, too. They take carbon dioxide from the air to help fuel their growth process, store carbon in their tissues, and put oxygen back into the atmosphere.

A mix of evergreen and deciduous trees is the best framework for any garden, but if there's only room in your garden for one tree, either choose a delicious variety of fruit tree or an ornamental tree with as many attributes as possible. Be sure to consider attractive shape, flowers, fruit, interesting leaf shape, bark texture, and foliage that is colorful all season or in fall or evergreen all year. A Japanese cherry will look fabulous with a huge cloud of pink or white blossom in spring, but it may be rather nondescript the rest of the year. Weeping trees, such as the silver-leaved weeping pear look wonderful all year, but they will need regular pruning. Conifers, on the other hand, provide a solid focal point and are relatively trouble free, but they are rather static.

Shapes of Trees

The shape of a tree is important. Trees may be rounded in form, open and spreading, narrow and columnar, cone-shaped or pyramidal, or weeping. The best tree shape for a particular location depends on what is around it. For example, if your garden is bordered by the straight horizontal lines of walls and buildings, consider planting a thin columnar (fastigiate)

LOOKING FOR A COLUMNAR SHAPE?

When you are seeking a columnar tree, look for the word *fastigiata* in the botanical name, or fastigiate in the plant's common name on the tag at the nursery or in catalog descriptions. Those terms describe a slender upright form.

Trees and Shrubs with Colored Foliage

Acer campestre 'Postelense', yellow hedge maple	*Gleditsia triacanthos* var. *inermis* 'Sunburst', thornless honey locust
Acer macrophyllum 'Mocha Rose', variegated bigleaf maple	*Hydrangea macrophylla* 'Lemon Wave'
Acer palmatum var. *atropurpureum* 'Bloodgood' and 'Moonfire', Japanese maple	*Hydrangea quercifolia* 'Little Honey', oakleaf hydrangea
Aucuba japonica, gold dust plant	*Kolkwitzia amabilis* 'Dream Catcher'
Cercis canadensis 'Forest Pansy', serviceberry	*Leucothoe fontanesiana* 'Girard's Rainbow'
Cornus mas 'Aurea', cornelian cherry	*Ligustrum* x *vicaryi*, golden vicary privet
Corylus maxima var. *purpurea*, purple giant filbert	*Liriodendron tulipifera* 'Aureo-marginatum'
Cotinus coggygria cvs., smokebush	*Philadelphus coronarius* 'Aureus', mock orange
Fagus sylvatica 'Atropunicea', 'Purple Fountain', and 'Purpurea Tricolor', European beech	*Physocarpus opulifolius* 'Dart's Golden', 'Coppertina', 'Diabolo', and 'Summer Wine', ninebark
Fraxinus americana 'Autumn Purple', white ash	*Spiraea japonica* 'Goldmound', Japanese spirea

When trees, especially aspens, cottonwoods, and sugar maples, show the undersides of their leaves, bad weather is coming.

tree or two to provide a strong vertical line. Some good columnar trees for North American gardens include Atlas cedar (*Cedrus atlantica* 'Fastigiata'), Washington hawthorn (*Crataegus phaenopyrum* 'Fastigiata'), white ash (*Fraxinus americana* 'Greenspire' and 'Manitoo'), eastern white pine (*Pinus strobus* 'Fastigata'), and giant arborvitae (*Thuja plicata* 'Fastigiata'). Some trees have such a striking shape they must stand alone as focal points, such as the tiered dogwood (*Cornus controversa*), which looks like a wedding cake.

ALLOW ENOUGH SPACE

Whatever size tree you plant, be sure to research what its eventual mature size will be, and leave enough space for the tree to grow to maturity comfortably. Too many gardeners make the mistake of planting trees too close to the house, only to end up moving or removing them when they grow too big for their space—an expensive and laborious undertaking.

Tree Shape Examples

Different tree shapes can add texture and dimension to your garden. Try to avoid using too many different shapes at once, because this will create a cluttered and disorganized look.

columnar (lombardy poplar)

V-shape (hackberry)

round (white oak)

pyramidal (pink oak)

oval (sugar maple)

Flowering trees include flowering cherry, witch hazel, and lilac.

Planting Considerations

In a large garden you have plenty of choices for trees. Try to include at least some native trees, not just because they will look at home but because they act as host to far more local insects and wildlife than exotic ornamentals. There are dozens of trees that are perfect for small gardens, but you must carefully consider your space and the final size of your tree. Watch out for the position of underground drains and cables close to where you are planning to plant trees, as well as above-ground wires and overhanging gutters and roofs. Also remember that a tree will sap nutrients from the surrounding area and restrict what is available for other plants. It may also throw considerable shade to deprive other plants of light.

Ornamental Qualities of Trees

When you know the tree shape that will work best in your planting location, consider what you'd like to see in the tree. If you want color, choose a tree with colored foliage or pretty flowers. If you love the warm tones of fall leaves, choose a tree that is known for rich fall color. To add interest to the landscape in winter, select an evergreen or a deciduous tree with interesting bark.

Plant Some Trees in Spring

It's okay to plant many trees in fall, but some are best planted in spring because they establish slowly in the soil. Plant these trees in spring: goldenrain tree (*Koelreuteria paniculata*), magnolias, most types of oaks, tulip tree (*Liriodendron tulipifera*), tupelo (*Nyssa sylvatica*), and Japanese zelkova (*Zelkova serrata*).

Avoid overwatering your trees and shrubs, because this can leave them damaged during the difficult winter period.

Water When It Matters Most

Most trees and shrubs can withstand some drought. But in late summer and fall, before the plants go into winter dormancy, water is important because they are setting buds for next year's leaves and flowers. Also the roots will not be able to take up water when the ground freezes in winter. If fall weather is dry, water your trees and shrubs deeply.

Trees with Attractive Bark	
Acer buergerianum, trident maple	*Pinus bungeana*, lacebark pine
Acer griseum, paperbark maple	*Platanus occidentalis*, American sycamore
Acer pensylvanicum, striped maple	*Prunus maackii*, Amur chokecherry
Betula nigra 'Heritage', river birch	*Stewartia pseudocamellia*, Japanese stewartia
Corylus columna, Turkish filbert	*Ulmus parviflora*, lacebark elm

Trees and Shrubs for Fall Color

Acer japonicum cvs., full moon maple	*Ginkgo biloba*, maidenhair tree
Acer palmatum var. *dissectum* cvs., Japanese maple	*Hamamelis* spp., witch hazel
Acer rubrum, red maple	*Hydrangea quercifolia*, oakleaf hydrangea
Acer saccharum, sugar maple	*Itea virginica* 'Henry's Garnet', sweetspire
Aronia arbutifolia, red chokeberry	*Lindera benzoin*, spicebush
Cladrastis kentukea, yellowwood	*Liquidambar styraciflua*, sweetgum
Clethra alnifolia, summersweet	*Nyssa sylvatica*, tupelo
Cornus spp., dogwood	*Oxydendrum arboreum*, sourwood
Crataegus spp., hawthorn	*Populus tremuloides*, quaking aspen
Enkianthus spp.	*Pyrus* spp., pear
Euonymus alatus, winged euonymus	*Quercus coccinea*, scarlet oak
Fothergilla spp.	*Rhus* spp., sumac
Fraxinus americana 'Autumn Purple'	*Sassafras albidum*

SHRUBS

Well-placed shrubs help provide the framework of a landscape, providing year-round height and structure. Shrubs can provide structural interest to punctuate beds of herbaceous perennials or annuals, they can provide shelter, year-round cover for wildlife, and you can choose shrubs that have wonderful foliage or flowers. Choose shrubs with an informal habit for a natural look in your landscape, or clip evergreens into formal shapes for a more designed look, which is perfect for an urban garden or formal setting. In a large landscape you can even mix and match the two styles.

Using Shrubs

Adding flowering shrubs to your garden is a great way to get lots of color without much work. Roses are the best known and best loved flowering shrubs, but there are many others. Some, like lilacs, daphnes, mock orange, and scented viburnums, such as Koreanspice viburnum (*Viburnum carlesii*), are wonderfully fragrant. Others, such as Japanese spirea and bigleaf hydrangea (especially newer varieties like Endless Summer) bloom for many weeks. Late in the season, some shrubs sport brilliant fall foliage or colorful fruit. In winter some show off colored stems. Shrubs are useful for hedges and informal screens, too. When you choose shrubs, don't overlook old-fashioned ones, such as deutzia, weigela, beautybush (*Kolkwitzia*), and lilacs—they are still wonderful additions to the landscape.

PLANT BY THE LILACS

Lilacs are a reliable guide to when it is safe to plant outdoors in spring. Here's how to use them:

Plant hardy annuals, such as sweet alyssum and pansies, and cool-season vegetables, such as peas and broccoli, when lilacs get their leaves.

Plant tender annuals, such as impatiens and marigolds, and warm-season vegetables, such as tomatoes, squash, and beans when lilacs are in full bloom.

Shrubs and Trees for Flowers

Aesculus x *carnea*, red horsechestnut	*Kolkwitzia amabilis*, beautybush
Aesculus spp., buckeye	*Laburnum* x *watereri*, goldenchain tree
Amelanchier spp., serviceberry	*Lagerstroemia indica*, crepe myrtle
Buddleia spp., butterfly bush	*Lindera benzoin*, spicebush
Caryopteris x *clandonensis*, blue-mist shrub	*Liriodendron tulipifera*, tulip tree
Cercis spp., redbud	*Lonicera* spp., honeysuckle
Chaenomeles speciosa, flowering quince	*Magnolia* spp.
Chionanthus spp., fringtree	*Malus* spp., flowering crabapple
Cladrastis kentukea, American yellowwood	*Oxydendrum arboreum*, sourwood
Clethra alnifolia, summersweet	*Philadelphus* cvs., mock orange
Cornus spp., dogwood	*Physocarpus opulifolius*, ninebark
Corylopsis spp., winterhazel	*Pieris japonica*, Japanese pieris
Cotinus spp., smokebush	*Potentilla fruticosa*, cinquefoil
Daphne spp.	*Prunus* spp., flowering cherry
Deutzia spp.	*Pyracantha coccinea*, firethorn
Forsythia spp.	*Pyrus* spp., pear
Fothergilla spp.	*Rhododendron* spp. and cvs., azalea and rhododendron
Franklinia alatamaha	*Rosa* cvs., roses
Halesia spp., silverbell	*Skimmia* spp.
Hamamelis spp., witch hazel	*Spiraea* spp., spirea
Hibiscus syriacus, rose of Sharon	*Stewartia pseudocamellia*
Hydrangea spp.	*Styrax* spp., snowbell
Hypericum spp., St. Johns wort	*Syringa* spp., lilac
Itea virginica, sweetspire	*Viburnum* spp.
Kalmia latifolia, mountain laurel	*Vitex agnus-castus*, chastetree
Kerria japonica, Japanese kerria	*Weigela florida*, old-fashioned weigela

HOW TO CHANGE HYDRANGEA COLOR

The color of many pink and blue varieties of bigleaf hydrangea (*Hydrangea macrophylla*) can vary with the soil pH. The blue color is due to aluminum in the soil, which becomes unavailable to plants in alkaline (high pH) soils. To turn a pink hydrangea blue, lower the soil pH around it by adding aluminum sulfate or garden sulfur. Organic matter helps, too. To turn a blue hydrangea pink, raise the soil pH by adding lime. Not all pink and blue hydrangeas will change color, but many will. White hydrangeas won't change their color with the pH.

ROSES

For many of us, a garden isn't complete if it doesn't contain roses. And the best part of a rose is the heavenly fragrance. Many modern rose varieties—hybrid teas, grandifloras, floribundas, and climbers—are bred for their color and form; they carry little or no scent. But go back a bit in rose history and you can find the lavishly perfumed heritage varieties—bourbons, damasks, centifolias, gallicas, and others. These old roses produce their big, full flowers on thorny shrubs. Some are tough and long-lived, but others are less hardy.

If fragrance is what you're after, either plant old rose varieties or try newer hybrids that combine the resilience of modern shrub roses with the full, richly fragrant flowers of the heritage varieties, such as David Austin English roses, which are widely available in a range of colors. Also look for Kordes roses, varieties bred by Wilhelm Kordes III, the fourth generation of a family of rose breeders.

Modern Landscape Roses

Shrub roses have really come into their own in recent years. There are now tough, hardy landscape roses that bloom all summer long, are resistant to black spot and mildew, and need little care. If you are willing to forgo fragrance for ease of maintenance, look for Knock Out, Flower Carpet, and Meidiland roses.

Gardeners in the northern United States and the majority of Canada can find extremely hardy roses that can take a lot of cold, such as Blanche Double de Coubert, Pierrette Pavement, and other rugosa varieties; Alexander MacKenzie, Austrian Copper, Captain Samuel Holland, and Henry Hudson.

NATURAL DISEASE PREVENTION

Black spot and powdery mildew are the bane of many a rosebush. Here's an effective, all-natural preventive spray you can make yourself. Dissolve 1 tablespoon of baking soda in 1 gallon (4 l) of water. Add a tablespoon of horticultural spray oil or insecticidal soap to help the spray stick to the leaves. Mix well and spray your roses every five to seven days in summer.

Shrubs and Trees with Colorful Fruit

Amelanchier spp. serviceberry	*Malus* spp., crabapple
Aronia arbutifolia, red chokeberry	*Myrica* spp., bayberry, wax myrtle
Callicarpa spp., beautyberry	*Prunus* spp., cherry, peach, plum
Chionanthus spp., fringetree	*Pyracantha* spp., firethorn
Cornus spp., dogwood	*Rhodotypos scandens*, jetbead
Cotoneaster spp.	*Rosa* spp., rose
Crataegus spp., hawthorn	*Sambucus* spp., elderberry
Elaeagnus multiflora, cherry elaeagnus	*Skimmia* spp.
Ilex spp., hollies	*Symphoricarpos albus*, snowberry
Ilex verticillata, winterberry	*Symplocos paniculata*, sapphireberry
Juniperus spp., juniper	*Vaccinium* spp., blueberry
Lindera benzoin, spicebush	*Vitis* spp., grape
Mahonia aquifolium, Oregon grapeholly	

THE EDIBLE GARDEN

One of the most satisfying aspects of gardening is growing your own food, and these days more and more people are catching the vegetable gardening bug, with good reason. There really is nothing like the flavor of a juicy, homegrown tomato or sugar snap peas that go from garden to stove in minutes. You can grow your own mesclun and sweet corn, raise your own basil for pesto, pick sweet strawberries at the peak of ripeness—all for far less than the cost of supermarket produce.

Food that is fresh and free from chemicals tastes utterly different from supermarket vegetables, which may have traveled halfway around the world before they get into your cart, and they have probably been doused in all sorts of chemicals to keep them fresh while they make that journey. So your own food is not only more delicious, it's better for you, too. This chapter also includes tips for storing your home-grown produce, so it's easy to enjoy the fruits of your labor long after the harvest.

GROW SOME VEGETABLES

It is a huge commitment to grow all your own fresh fruit and vegetables, and to be entirely self-sufficient, you would need plenty of space. However, it is no trouble to grow a few things, and you can eat your own salads, herbs, and some vegetables, even if you only have a windowbox and a few pots or a small balcony garden. Small steps often lead to great strides, and you may soon find yourself digging a garden in the backyard or renting a plot in a local community garden.

Another advantage to vegetable gardening is that you don't need to know much to get going. With a packet of mixed salad seed, a bag of potting mix and a container, which could be anything from a terra-cotta or glazed ceramic pot to a wooden box or even a plastic tub with holes poked in the bottom, you can pick your own salad greens for weeks or even months. You can grow a potato plant in compost in an old plastic trash can, and Jerusalem artichokes will grow in any average soil.

A LOT FOR NOT VERY MUCH

One packet of mixed salad seed can provide the equivalent of 20 bags of salad from a supermarket. Quick and easy, they'll grow in large pots and tubs as well as in the vegetable plot.

PLANNING YOUR VEGETABLE GARDEN

Before you decide how much space you need or how you want your kitchen garden to look, think carefully about what you like to eat. There is no point in growing everything unless you are embarking on self-sufficiency. More vegetable gardens fail because people start by growing too much, rather than too little. It is disheartening if your radishes get woody, your spinach bolts, your peas wither,

GETTING STARTED

All you need to get started growing your own vegetables are some different-sized pots, a bag of potting mix, a hand fork, a trowel, and a watering can.

if your broccoli gets eaten by bugs, and your zucchini turn into baseball bats before you pick them. If you look forward to eating your vegetables, you'll probably keep a close eye on your garden. The other common mistake is to end up with a glut of something that you just can't eat; this usually means you have chosen the wrong vegetable. So let your tastebuds be your guide when deciding what to grow.

An Abundance of Choices

Salads greens are easy to grow, fast to mature, and easy to use. Some salad greens are also very ornamental. They come in many different shades of green and there are red-leaved lettuce varieties, frilly mizuna and endive, and stately mustard greens. So a few salad crops are a must for most gardens. Leafy greens, such as spinach and chard are also easy to grow and fast to mature, so they are good for beginning gardeners. Brassicas—cabbage, broccoli, cauliflower, and Brussels sprouts—take a long time to mature and can be magnets for troublesome pests, so they are probably not the ideal choice for new gardeners. Onions and potatoes take up a lot of space and are easily available in stores and markets, so it's not worth growing a lot of them unless you have plenty of room. The one thing most gardeners want to grow is their own tomatoes; there are varieties for everyone, from tumbling forms for hanging baskets to rangy outdoor plants to neat bushes. Herbs and strawberries are also happy in pots or hanging baskets and, if space is a real consideration, many vegetables grow well in pots. You can grow salad and herb crops in a windowbox or even on an indoor sill.

Peas and beans are easy to grow; bush varieties don't need staking, but pole beans produce over a longer time. Zucchini and other summer squash are easy to grow once they get past the first stages, but don't be tempted to plant too many—two or three healthy plants will feed a family for a month; half a dozen will feed a small village.

The other thing to remember as you dream of eating your homegrown vegetables is maintenance. If you are always away for a month in August, only grow varieties that produce their crop early—salad greens, spinach, bush beans, peas, carrots, radishes, and beets, for example. Forget about tomatoes, peppers, zucchini, and eggplant unless you have someone who can come in every day to water and check them for you.

Frost is more likely when the moon is new or full.

SHORT ON TIME?

If you are a weekend gardener with no time during the week, choose low-maintenance vegetables that don't need much staking, watering, or weeding. Bush beans, chard, and radishes are a few undemanding and tasty choices.

Beans are easy to grow. You just need to make sure the vines have stable support and get plenty of water.

DESIGNS FOR EASY MAINTENANCE

Choose a sunny spot for the garden. Most vegetables need full sun, though some, including salad greens, broccoli, cabbage, carrots, beets, chard, spinach, kale, and rhubarb, will cope with shade. Pick an area where the ground is as level as possible. If you have sloping ground, think about making raised beds, which run across the slope and are filled with good soil about 12 inches (30 cm) deep, preferably on a thick base of compost. Even if you have lots of space, raised beds are a great way of growing vegetables, providing a good depth of soil and good drainage. They are the best solution if you have heavy clay soil.

Drainage is important in flat and raised beds because the roots need oxygen as well as moisture.

If your property is small, you don't need to have a dedicated vegetable garden. Instead work vegetables into whatever space you can find. Grow salads as edging along beds, grow climbing vegetables up trellises and teepees, and when you have a spare square foot of soil, make the most of the space by mixing quick-cropping vegetables, such as salads, radishes, and scallions between rows of longer maturing ones, such as shell beans, peppers, cabbage, and tomatoes.

Rows or Beds?

There's no ideal size for a kitchen garden, but you can grow a significant amount of food in a plot about 10 x 20 feet (3 x 6 m). You can lay out your garden in single or wide rows with space between them or group the plants into beds. A square or rectangular plot is easiest to manage. If you opt for rows, make them straight so you can easily hoe between them. A spiraling row of peas or a drift of carrots may look pretty but will be a nightmare to weed. Many gardeners prefer to divide a vegetable plot into distinct narrow beds. The ideal width for a bed is approximately 4 feet (1 m) so you can easily reach in to weed from either side without stepping on the soil. If you have space, divide your vegetable area into four or six distinct beds or sections to make it easier to plan crop rotations.

A path between beds needs to be wide enough to push a wheelbarrow comfortably—at least 3 feet (1 m). If you don't have space for this, at least leave enough space to kneel on the ground to weed without damaging plants. It is also helpful to have your compost bin somewhere close by. Then you can cut off stalks and leaves that you won't eat before taking the vegetables into the kitchen, and throw any trimmings straight into the compost. You also can get finished compost easily from bin to bed.

Soil in raised beds needs to be forked and spread with compost before planting and then again every spring for maintenance.

Weeds in your vegetable patch can be kept under control, if you weed little and often, either by hand or by working between the rows with a hoe.

CROP ROTATION

Rotating the vegetables you plant from year to year prevents the buildup of pests, such as bean beetles, and soil-borne diseases that attack a particular crop. It's a way of helping one crop to benefit from the previous one. When you're starting out, don't worry too much about rotation, since your choices of vegetables will probably change from year to year. Just make sure that you don't grow exactly the same crop in the same place for more than two years, and keep your plants healthy by keeping them well fed and watered.

When you are planning rotations, you want to plant heavy-feeding vegetables that require nutrient-rich soil one year, then follow with light-feeding plants the next year. The third year, plant crops that help build the soil by fixing nitrogen in it. If you have a large garden, plan out your crop rotations on paper so you don't get confused from year to year. And continue to add compost and organic fertilizers to all the beds or rows every year.

An important reason not to grow crops in the same place is to fool the pests that prey on those crops. For example, potatoes are prey to wireworm, a soil pest that chews on roots, tubers, and seeds and can affect many other vegetables and flowers if it gets established. If

Keep a record of your crop rotation schedule to make sure your soil nutrients are not depleted.

Nutrient Needs of Vegetables

Heavy Feeders	Lettuce	Onions
Asparagus	Okra	Parsnips
Beets	Radishes	Peppers
Broccoli	Rhubarb	Potatoes
Brussels sprouts	Spinach	Shallots
Cabbage, Chinese cabbage	Summer squash	Sweet potatoes
Cauliflower	Tomatoes	Turnips, rutabagas
Celery	Winter squash, pumpkins	
Collard greens		**Nitrogen Fixers**
Corn	**Light Feeders**	Alfalfa
Cucumbers	Carrots	Beans, all types
Eggplant	Chard	Clover
Endive and escarole	Garlic	Peanuts
Kale	Leeks	Peas
Kohlrabi	Mustard greens	Soybeans

you move spuds around your plot each year, the wireworm never gets the chance to get established. However, if it does it's really hard to eliminate.

VEGETABLE GARDEN BASICS

If you've never grown vegetables before, start with the easiest ones. Don't try to grow rows of perfect celeriac or cabbages in year one; instead, stick to vegetables that give you the best return for the least effort.

Some vegetables grow best when sown directly in the garden, either because they are hardy and can go into the ground early or they don't transplant well. Gardeners in cool climates can get a head start on warm-season vegetables, such as tomatoes and eggplant by starting seeds indoors and moving the seedlings out when the weather is warm and frost danger is past.

Start with Salads

Everyone can grow salad greens. Start with cut-and-come-again varieties that keep on going: One sowing and you can cut a few leaves at a time for weeks. Classic cut-and-come-again varieties include leaf lettuce, such as Salad Bowl, Oak Leaf, and Lollo Rosso, frisée, mache, cress, sorrel, and mizuna. Rocket, or arugula, grows as fast as its name suggests, so you can mix it with any salad sowing. Ruby and Rainbow chard are pretty

DON'T SPREAD DISEASE

Many plant diseases are spread by contact, so always wash your hands (or your gardening gloves) after working around diseased plants. Sterilize your tools by dipping them in a 10 percent solution of liquid household chlorine bleach and water. Rinse and dry the tools before you use them.

Salad Vegetables

Some of the easiest vegetables to grow are those you might think of as salad vegetables. Tomatoes, lettuce, chard, peas, beans, and spinach all make good projects for the beginner gardener.

Tomatoes need some support struts and can be grown in containers.

Chard should be sown in spring for picking during the summer.

Peas like a sunny area with a lot of moisture and heavy compost.

Lettuce grows best in cooler climates.

Spinach can be sown in spring for a summer crop, or in fall for winter picking.

Beans need a sheltered spot away from strong winds.

Easy to Grow Vegetables

These vegetables are easy to grow and quick to mature.

Arugula	Mustard greens
Beets	Peas
Bush snap beans	Radishes
Chard	Scallions
Garden cress	Spinach
Kale	Summer squash
Leaf lettuce	Turnips

Sow your seeds in straight lines to keep your garden care and maintenance as simple as possible.

and can be harvested as tiny salad leaves as well as full-grown leaves. An even easier way to grow your own salads is to use a mesclun or salad greens seed mix—many different blends are available.

Radishes are the perfect fast-growing starter crop to encourage grown-up salad-lovers and get children interested in gardening. You don't need to stick with traditional red-and-white radishes; there are also long, short, dark, pale, sweet, and very hot varieties. Once you've realized how easy it is to grow salad, move on to crisphead and Romaine lettuces; try pak choi, tatsoi, and mibuna. You'll never need to buy a bag of salad at the supermarket again!

Direct-Sow or Transplant?

Sow Directly in the Garden	Parsnips	Collard greens
Beans	Spinach	Eggplant
Corn	Squash and pumpkins	Endive, escarole
Okra	Turnips	Garlic
Peanuts		Kale
Peas	**Transplant Easily**	Kohlrabi
	Arugula	Leeks
Transplant with Care	Beet	Lettuce
Artichoke	Broccoli	Mustard greens
Beets	Brussels sprouts	Onions
Carrots	Cabbage	Peppers
Chard	Cauliflower	Shallots
Cucumbers	Celery	Tomatoes

Sowing Bean Seeds in Pots

Some beans, such as runner beans, have a high germination rate. To make sure you get enough—but not too many—seedlings, start your beans in pots.

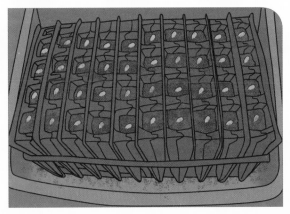

Plant your seeds about six to eight weeks before the last killing frost.

Plant your seedlings about one to two weeks before the last killing frost.

Prevent Pests and Diseases

To minimize threats from pests and diseases, build good, rich soil in your kitchen garden. Allow for good air circulation around plants. Keep the garden clean—pull the weeds, and remove leaves and other debris promptly.

Avoid Chemical Fertilizers

These provide your vegetables with nitrogen in the form of nitrates as salt. Avoid them because they will burn the roots of your vegetables and reduce the quality of all your harvest.

Sow More Than You Need

Sow more vegetable seeds than you need and assume that some of them won't germinate. When the seedlings come up, be prepared to get rid of the extras and thin the rest to leave the sturdiest plants at the proper spacing.

Sow in Succession

Sow salads in succession, starting a new batch every three or four weeks in early spring to make sure you have a constant supply of fresh leaves. Harvest by cutting the outer leaves when they are big enough to eat.

CARROTS AND PARSNIPS

Carrots and parsnips become forked and misshapen in rich soil; don't add manure or other high-nitrogen fertilizers to their bed.

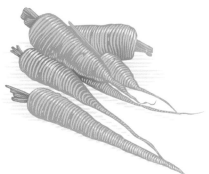

Carrots grow best in light, sandy soil and mature in 12 to 16 weeks.

NATURAL SUPPORT

Grow pole beans with corn or sunflowers, like Native Americans did. The stalks support the bean vines.

VEGETABLE GARDEN FAVORITES

When the hot days of summer arrive, nothing tastes better than a juicy, ripe tomato fresh from the garden. Peppers and cucumbers are part of summer gardens, too. Plant them when the weather warms in spring so you can enjoy them when summer hits its peak. And in addition to beans and summer squash, fresh-from-the-garden sweet corn is always popular.

Beans

Beans are easy to grow, delicious, versatile in the kitchen, and good for us, too. There are green, yellow, or purple snap beans (or string beans) to eat pod and all, shell beans to eat fresh or dried, and novelties like yard-long beans. Pole beans grow on long vines that need to climb up strings, netting, trellises, or teepees. Bush beans have shorter stems that in most cases will stand up on their own. Some bean plants have pretty flowers, too—Scarlet Runner beans have bright red blossoms, and Royalty Purple Pod has purple flowers. Many old-time bean varieties are regional favorites that have been grown for generations in different places. Look for these heirlooms in the catalogs of small regional seed companies and groups like the Seed Savers Exchange (find them at www.seedsavers.org).

Some Heirloom Bean Varieties

Dragon's Tongue—bush yellow snap bean with purple markings	Lazy Housewife—pole green snap
	Marvel of Venice—pole yellow snap
Empress—bush green snap	Painted Pony—bush green snap or dried shell bean
Garden of Eden—pole green snap	Royalty Purple Pod—pole purple snap
Jacob's Gold—bush shell bean	Tiger's Eye—bush fresh or dried shell
Kentucky Wonder—pole green snap	Tongue of Fire—fresh shell

Summer Squash

Zucchini and other summer squash are legendary producers. Their fruit is delicious in a platter of crudités, or sautéed, baked, broiled, grilled, or steamed. Start seeds indoors and transplant outdoors when all danger of frost is past and the soil has warmed. Space vining varieties 6 feet (2 m) apart and bush varieties 4 feet (1.2 m) apart. The traditional way to plant squash is in a small mound of soil 4 inches (10 cm) high. Sow six seeds in each hill and thin to leave the strongest two seedlings.

Plants have both male and female flowers, and pollination is critical for fruit production. If bees and other insects are scarce in your garden,

Zucchini is a great producer, so you will probably need only 2 or 3 healthy plants for a whole crop.

use a clean artist's paintbrush to transfer pollen from male to female flowers. (Female flowers have a swelling right behind the blossom that will become the fruit; male flowers don't have the bump.)

Bigger isn't better where summer squash are concerned. Pick your zucchini while they're still young and relatively small. If you let them grow to baseball-bat size they will be tough and seedy.

Sweet Corn

Corn is synonymous with summer. There are yellow, white, and bicolored varieties with varying degrees of sweetness. For old-fashioned corn flavor, grow "normal sugary" varieties, and cook them as soon as possible after picking, because their sugar converts rapidly into starch and that "fresh-picked" flavor begins to decline. "Sugary enhanced" corn varieties are more tender and a bit sweeter. Sweetest of all are "super sweet" varieties, which convert their sugar to starch slowly after picking, but aren't as tender as sugary enhanced corn. "Synergistic" varieties combine sugary enhanced and supersweet kernels.

Plant corn in blocks for best pollination, with plants 9 inches (23 cm) apart in rows 3 feet (1 m) apart; you will need at least four rows. When the silks turn brown, it's time to pick the corn. Make sure it's ready by performing the thumbnail test (below right).

BEAT THE BORER

The dreaded squash vine borer is the bane of many a zucchini. The larva of an orange-and-black moth with clear wings, the borer is about 1 inch (2.5 cm) long and white with a dark head. It chews the base of stems in early summer and goes on into other parts of the plant. If your squash plants wilt suddenly, look for borers in the stems. If you find one, slit the stem, remove and destroy the larva, then cover the damaged part of the stem with dirt. With luck, the plant will keep on growing.

Plant your corn when the oak leaves are as big as a mouse's ear.

EASY-TO-GROW RELATIVES

Chard is the easiest leafy green to grow; it germinates easily, you can use the small leaves and thinnings for salads, and it produces all summer long and into fall. Lots of gardeners grow it instead of spinach, because it keeps cropping long after spinach has bolted. Beets are a close relative of chard (their leaves are edible, too) and are another easy vegetable to grow. Varieties include sweet golden types, striped pink and white, and cylindrical or torpedo-shaped ruby-colored roots that are easy to slice.

THUMBNAIL TEST FOR CORN

To be sure corn is ripe, pull back a few leaves to uncover part of an ear and press your fingernail into it. If milky juice spurts out, the corn is ready. If the kernels contain no liquid, the corn is past its peak.

Brandywine and Yellow Brandywine tomatoes are popular varieties.

Tomatoes

Tomatoes are probably every gardener's favorite vegetable and one chosen by many beginners. Starting your garden is a great opportunity to choose really tasty heirloom varieties that you can't find in stores or garden centers, so be sure to check out seed catalogs offering these old-fashioned varieties.

Growing Tomatoes Tomatoes grow in either of two ways: they are indeterminate, or vining, meaning that the plants continue to grow and bear fruit until frost shuts them down; or they are determinate, bushy plants that grow to a certain height and then stop, producing their crop over a shorter period of time. Within those two basic categories there are big beefsteak types, round-fruited types, smaller patio varieties, oblong paste, or Roma, varieties, and small cherry and grape tomatoes. In addition to the typical red fruits, there are also orange and yellow tomatoes. Some modern varieties (labeled VFN) are resistant to diseases, such as verticillium and fusarium wilt, and to nematodes, tiny soil-dwelling pests. Older heirloom varieties have marvelous flavor but are less resistant to disease.

Tomatoes grow best in rich soil with even moisture. Start seeds indoors several weeks before the last frost date and move seedlings into the garden when they are no more than 12 inches (30 cm) high, and the soil is warm.

Grow Some Heirlooms It's fun to grow some heirloom varieties; you could plant several different varieties and conduct your own tomato tasting when the crop comes in. Check the catalogs of regional seed companies or the Seed Savers Exchange to find heirloom tomato varieties.

A Dozen Heirloom Tomatoes

Amish Paste	Hungarian Heart
Black Prince	Moscovich
Brandywine	Pruden's Purple
Cherokee Green	Red Pear Piriform
Great White	Rose
Green Zebra	Striped German

Removing Sideshoots

As indeterminate tomato varieties grow you can remove the side shoots that appear between the main stem and each fruiting branch. If you leave them on they divert energy, which needs to be heading for the fruit. This pruning also allows more sunlight to reach the fruit. Just grasp the side shoots firmly and bend them sharply downward to break them cleanly from the branch. Remember to do it while the shoots are small, before they get out of control. You'll still get a tomato crop without removing the shoots, but it will be smaller.

Side shoots can be planted separately to grow more tomato plants and an even larger crop.

Peppers

Peppers divide into two basic groups: sweet peppers (which start out green, then ripen to red, orange, yellow, or purple) and hot peppers (which range in heat from the mild Anaheim to the incendiary Habanero.)

Peppers need warm, sunny weather to thrive. They are very sensitive to frost, although they are said to produce the most fruit when exposed to cool temperatures as young plants. Start seeds indoors two months before your last frost date and transplant into the garden after frost danger is past and the weather is warm. Give them fertile soil that is well drained; keep it evenly moist.

You can pick your peppers when they are green or let them ripen. Sweet peppers are sweeter when fully ripe; hot peppers are hotter. Keep them picked and the plants will keep on producing more as long as the weather is warm.

Scoville Units The heat of hot peppers is measured in Scoville units, a scale developed by Wilbur Scoville in the early 1900s. He figured out a way to measure the amount of capsaicin in hot peppers. Pure capsaicin comes in at 15,000,000 units on the Scoville scale. By comparison, bell peppers measure 0, Anaheim comes in at 500 to 2,500 Scoville units, Jalapeño at 2,500 to 4,500, Cayenne at 30,000 to 50,000 units, and Habanero hits 100,000 to 325,000 on the Scoville scale.

Sweet peppers grow on bushy plants up to 30 inches (75 cm) tall.

CUT, DON'T PULL, PEPPERS

To harvest peppers, cut the fruit from the plant with a sharp knife or pruners. Don't pull off the fruit or you may damage the brittle stem and harm the plant.

Growing cucumbers on a trellis helps to ensure that you harvest an undamaged crop.

A cloche is a row cover for protecting plants in cooler temperatures and winds.

Cucumbers

Cucumbers grow on sprawling vines or shorter vines (called bush varieties) and are meant for either pickling or slicing. They are very frost sensitive and need warm weather. A sunny location in rich soil is ideal; enrich the planting area with plenty of compost and fertilizer. Start seeds indoors three to four weeks before the last frost date and move plants into the garden when all frost danger is past and the soil is warm.

Transplant with care—cucumbers don't like to be moved, but they will tolerate it if you handle them gently.

If you train the vines to climb a trellis instead of letting them sprawl across the ground, the fruit will be straight and probably won't be attacked by slugs or develop rot from contact with the ground. They'll also take up less space. Make sure the plants get plenty of water while they are blooming and developing their fruit.

Harvest cucumbers when they are big enough to use. Be sure to pick them before they start to turn yellow—unless you are growing a yellow variety.

A LATE HARVEST

You'll know you've become a serious gardener when you're picking your own vegetables in fall and beyond. You can leave some crops, such as leeks, right in the garden, heavily mulched, and dig them after the weather turns cold. Polytunnels and cold frames let you grow cold-hardy greens and other vegetables to harvest while the cold winds blow. Cloches create warm environments for individual plants. See "Extending the Growing Season" (page 168) for information on making and using these devices.

When the temperature falls below freezing and stays there, close up the cold frame for the winter. Whenever daytime temperatures climb above freezing, open the lid of the frame to let in fresh air and check the plants to be sure they are not drying out. Harvest by picking the outer leaves of the plants as they grow big enough to use.

Plants to Grow

Even the best cold frame won't let you grow tomatoes in January in the North. Instead, plant cool-weather vegetables in your late-season garden.

Sow before the end of September to make sure there is enough light and warmth for seeds to germinate. Make sure your soil is well drained; plants will freeze if they are left to stand with their roots in pools of water.

Grow cut-and-come again crops and Chinese greens rather than delicate summer lettuces.

Winter salad leaves are tougher than summer ones and often have a robust flavor that can sometimes be a little bitter. To avoid this, try blanching the leaves by covering the plants with an upturned flowerpot. Leave the plants like this for a few days before harvesting and leaves will become paler and less bitter.

WINTER SALAD GREENS

Choose hardy varieties of your favorite summer salad greens or experiment with more unusual crops. Winter salad greens are the ideal substitute when you can't satisfy your craving for tomatoes and fresh summer salad, but need the crunch of fresh green vegetables.

Endives survive winter outside in warm climates but need the protection of a cold frame in cooler climates.

Garden cress tastes like watercress and matures within two months.

Golden purslane—the red stems look wonderful against the golden leaves and will brighten up a salad bowl.

Kale develops a sweeter flavor when grown in cold weather.

Mache, or corn salad, will survive cold weather, but sow before mid-September because it grows slowly.

Oriental greens, such as Pak Choi, Green in Snow mustard, and Wintertime Chinese cabbage grow well in an insulated cold frame in winter. Flavors range from peppery and pungent to mild and sweet.

Radicchio sown in late September produce sweet, deep maroon leaves.

Texel greens—leaves taste like spinach, and they can be used in stir-fries or salads.

Winter purslane or miner's lettuce (Claytonia)— hardy, green, and tasty; sow the seed of this salad leaf in August and September for salad throughout the winter.

Frost is not likely in fall when the soil is warm and wet.

For a continuous supply of winter greens, sow your seeds every 4 weeks.

Storing Root Vegetables

Although a freezer is useful for storing most produce, it isn't suitable for keeping root vegetables at their best. You can keep beets, carrots, and parsnips for months in cool, dry storage, and there's no need to wash your harvest beforehand. The important thing to remember is to remove any damaged or rotting vegetables from the batch or they will ruin your entire crop.

1 Lift root vegetables in early winter before serious frosts.

2 Twist off foliage near the crown.

3 Pack in boxes in layers with sand between them and covering the top layer.

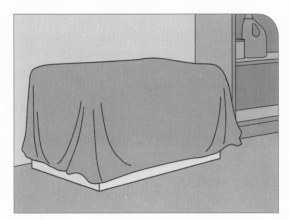

4 Store in a garage or cool dark place, but don't let them freeze—cover the boxes with blankets or sacks in freezing weather.

COMPANION PLANTING

Serious gardeners used to turn their noses up at companion planting, seeing it as folklore rather than horticulture. However, for many longtime gardeners it is an effective way of keeping plants healthy by growing different groups of plants together. Companion planting is based on centuries of gardeners' observations of which plants seem to be good neighbors in the garden and which ones don't seem to grow well together. Growing different plants together can offer their companions protection by attracting beneficial insects or acting as a decoy for harmful pests. Tall plants can also protect shorter ones, stiff stems can act as supports for more delicate twining ones, sturdy plants can offer wind protection, and those with generous foliage can offer shade and weed protection.

Umbellifers, plants with flat spreading heads of flowers, such as fennel and dill, attract hoverflies and other beneficial insects that feed on pests, such as aphids. Plant these among your vegetables to keep bad bugs down.

Planting to Attract Helpful Insects

Make space in or around your vegetable patch for plants that attract helpful insects that feed on pests.

Anise (*Pimpinella anisum*)	Dill (*Anethum graveolens*)
Buckwheat (*Fagopyron esculentum*)	Fennel (*Foeniculum vulgare*)
Candytuft (*Iberis* spp.)	Goldenrod (*Solidago* spp.)
Caraway (*Carum carvi*)	Morning glory (*Ipomoea* spp.)
Coriander (*Coriandrum sativum*)	Phacelia (*Phacelia tanacetifolia*)
Cornflower/knapweed (*Centaurea* spp.)	Meadow foam (*Limnanthes douglasii*)

Companion Plants to Grow

Marigolds exude a substance from their roots that discourages soil pests, such as nematodes, and they are said to keep away aphids and other aboveground pests, as well as repel Colorado potato beetles from potato plants. Don't plant them near beans; they are believed to interfere with the growth of bean plants.

Onions, garlic, leeks, chives, and other alliums are planted to repel insects. They are considered good companions for carrots, tomatoes, grapes, and roses. Keep them away from peas and beans.

Rue seems to deter beetles, fleas, and aphids, but it is harmful to cabbage. If you grow it, wear gloves when handling or working around it; its leaves can cause severe skin irritation.

Sage is grown near cabbage to repel cabbage worms and deter root maggots. It is also considered a good companion for carrots, tomatoes, and strawberries. Keep it away from cucumbers.

Do not plant anything between last quarter and new moon. This is a good time to pull weeds.

Trap Crops

Some companions are planted because pests love them; the plants serve as decoys to lure pests away from the plants you want to protect. Castor bean (*Ricinus communis*) and chrysanthemums attract nematodes. Black nightshade (*Solanum nigrum*) draws Colorado potato beetles. Nasturtiums are among aphids' favorite plants, so plant blocks of them to decoy the bugs away from other areas of your vegetable garden.

Good Vegetable Companions

These plants are traditionally grown together:

Asparagus—plant with carrots and tomatoes	Nasturtium—beans, brassicas, lettuce, strawberries
Beets—cabbage, salad greens, kohlrabi, onions	Onions—beets, brassicas, lettuce, sage
Brassicas (cabbage, broccoli, cauliflower, Brussels sprouts, collards, kale)—beans, celery, onions, potatoes	Peas—carrots, corn, cucumbers, eggplant, lettuce, peppers, radishes, spinach, tomatoes
Carrots—cucumbers, leeks, onions, peas, radishes	Peppers—carrots, onions
Corn—beans, cucumbers, melons, peas, squash	Potatoes—beans, corn, lettuce, onions, radishes
Cucumber—beans, broccoli, cabbage, corn, lettuce, onions, radishes, tomatoes	Radishes—beans, brassicas, carrots, lettuce, onions, peas, tomatoes
Garlic—brassicas, eggplant, tomatoes	Squash—beans, corn, radishes
Lettuce—beets, cabbage, radishes, strawberries	Tomatoes—asparagus, brassicas, carrots, onions

Doubtless God could have made a better berry, but doubtless God never did.

—Izaak Walton

SOFT FRUIT

Even a tiny garden can find space for strawberries, but they do need sun and protection. Raspberries need a bit of space. Blueberries are easy to grow, if your soil is acidic.

Strawberries

Strawberries are the perfect starter fruits; varieties are available that are happy in tubs, windowboxes, and hanging baskets as well as in open ground. Small, sweet, intensely flavored red or white alpine strawberries will colonize your garden if you give them half a chance. Everbearing strawberries will produce fruit two or three times over the course of the growing season, and day-neutral varieties also produce over a longer time than traditional June-bearing varieties.

Either grow strawberries in tall pots or give them a dedicated bed, if possible. Mulch the plants with straw as soon as they start to fruit to keep the fruit above ground and prevent disease, rot, and pest problems. You can prune the plants in summer or fall after the crop has been picked and remove the runners, or leave them in place, depending on which growing method you are using. For a new crop, separate the runners in late spring to start new plants, or put in new plants from the nursery as soon as the soil can be worked in spring.

Raspberries

The easiest raspberries for beginners or busy gardeners are everbearing varieties. Simply cut the whole plant right down to the ground after fruiting. Summer-fruiting varieties need to have the spent canes cut down after fruiting and new shoots tied to a frame. Many gardeners use a series of horizontal wires fastened to posts to train the raspberry canes. Boysenberries, tayberries, and loganberries need to be treated in a similar way; these all fruit on the previous year's growth. After fruiting, cut the old shoots back to the ground and fasten the following season's fruiting shoots to the frame in fall. As they grow in spring, keep tying the shoots to the frame. Raspberries and the hybrid berries like their roots covered with a thick mulch of compost or well-rotted manure.

Blueberries

Blueberries fall into two main groups, according to where they are grown. Rabbiteye berries (*Vaccinium ashei*) are native to the southeastern United States and do well in the hot, humid conditions there. Highbush blueberries (*Vaccinium corymbosum* and *V. australe*) grow in the East and North in well-drained, acidic soils. The plants are deciduous bushes that are planted in spring. Plant two or more varieties together to ensure cross-pollination. Plant rabbiteye plants 7–8 feet (2.1–2.4 m) apart and highbush 6 feet (1.8 m) apart.

When you are planting, cut back plants by one-quarter and prune off any bushy growth around the base of the plants. After two to three years of growth, prune upright bushes to open up the center and spreading bushes to remove low, shaded branches. Remove old branches six years old or more to encourage young, vigorous, growth. Prune off any shoots that grow in late summer.

Make several pickings in summer as the berries ripen.

Potted strawberries need central as well as the standard base drainage. Place a plastic tube in the center of the pot and fill with drainage material. Remove the tube after you have added the compost.

COMPANION PLANTING FOR FRUIT

You can practice companion planting with fruit, too. Blackberries grow well with grapes, and grapes like to be near beans and peas. Peaches grow well near asparagus, grapes, garlic, and onions. Plant beans, lettuce, or spinach near strawberries.

HOW TO GET THE BIGGEST BLUEBERRIES

Wait up to six days after blueberries turn blue to pick them; they continue to get bigger for several days after they appear ripe.

Cherry trees may need to be planted in pairs.

FRUIT TREES

Apple trees are understandably the most popular of all fruit trees, and if you can only have one kind of fruit tree, choose from hundreds of tasty apple varieties. Excellent varieties have been developed to grow in containers or on patios as well as dwarf and semidwarf varieties to grow in the landscape. You can also find old-fashioned heirloom apples with wonderful flavor. There is sure to be an apple tree to suit your garden, provided you can find some sun and shelter from strong winds.

If you have space for fruit trees, consider cherries, pears, or plums. Peaches and apricots can be prone to peach leaf curl, which is a virus spread by rain, they grow best in drier or sheltered gardens.

The main factors influencing your choice of fruit tree, apart from taste, are size and situation. In a small garden, espaliered fruit trees can save loads of space. Espaliered trees are trained on heavy wires to grow in a flat plane, with the branches forming U shapes, horizontal or angled straight lines (called cordons), or splayed out in fan shapes. Espaliers can be grown against walls and fences or trained against supports.

AVOID FROST POCKETS

Don't plant fruit trees at the bottom of a slope. Cold air rolls down a slope like water and pools at the bottom to create chilly pockets where frost lingers. The cold conditions can damage fruit tree blossoms and ruin the harvest.

A Dozen Heirloom Apples

Ashmead's Kernel	Rhode Island Greening
Cox's Orange Pippin	Roxbury Russet
Gravenstein	Smokehouse
Lady	Spitzenberg
Maiden's Blush	Tydeman's Early
Pink Pearl	Winter Banana

Size is a major factor when choosing your fruit tree. A potted apple tree might be the right size for your medium-size garden, but be sure to check how large the tree will grow and into what shape. You don't want it to dwarf your space.

Espaliers allow your fruit tree to collect as much light, water, and nutrients as a regular plant, but it forms a two-dimensional shape that takes up far less space and can be grown against a wall.

If you have more space and want to grow a small orchard, there are several ways to arrange the trees. You can map out the space in a grid and plant one tree in the center of each square. Or you can lay out the space in equilateral triangles, with a tree in each corner of the triangle. If you are growing dwarf trees, you can plant them in a double row to form a hedgerow. Just be sure to leave enough space between them to allow access for harvesting, pruning, and other maintenance.

Dwarf and semidwarf fruit trees have the top, fruit-producing, part of the tree grafted onto a rootstock that determines the overall size and vigor of the tree. For example, an apple tree on a very dwarfing rootstock may grow to an eventual height and spread of 5 feet (1.5 m) while the same variety of apple on a vigorous rootstock can grow into a large tree over 20 feet (6.5 m) in height and spread.

Some fruit trees are self-fertile, or self-fruitful, and will produce a good crop on their own. Most, however, require or will benefit from a pollination partner. This will be a different variety of the same fruit species, which flowers at about the same time.

Commercial potting soil is suitable for growing fruit trees in containers, but it should be loose enough to permit proper drainage.

Self-Fruitful Apple Varieties

These apples do not require a pollinator variety in order to bear fruit:

Grimes Golden	Stark Golden Delicious
Jon-A-Red	Starkspur Red Rome Beauty
Jonathan	Yellow Delicious

Cherries

Sweet red, yellow, and black cherries are among the great treats of summer. Tart red sour cherries are unbeatable for baking pies. Some sweet cherries require two different varieties to produce fruit, but some varieties are incompatible with one another. If you decide to grow sweet cherries, ask the nursery whether you need a pollinator and, if so, which it should be for your chosen variety. Happily, sour cherries are self-fruitful, and you can plant just one tree and get a crop.

Cherry trees bloom fairly early in spring, and late cold snaps can damage them in northern climates, so be cautious in planting them if you live where spring weather tends to swing back and forth between warm and cold.

Wassail the trees,
that they may beare,
You many a Plum
and many a Peare;
For more or less
Fruits they will bring,
As you doe give
them Wassailing.

—Robert Herrick

Lavender has a distinctive scent and is popular dried.

THE HERB GARDEN

People have always used herbs. Throughout history herbs have been used for medicine, to preserve and flavor food, and to make dyes for fabric, as well as for their scent. Herbs shouldn't be confined to the kitchen. Establish a herb garden to find dozens of uses for these charming plants, for healing, medicinal teas, for fragrant potpourris and sachets, in baths, and as cut and dried flowers. Herbs can be broadly divided into perennials and annuals, with a few biennials for good measure.

Perennial Herbs

The perennials are the permanent parts of the herb garden, taking you right through the year. Oregano, lavender, rosemary, and sages should be in everyone's garden, for their scent, their appearance, and to attract insects and bees, as well as for cooking and household uses. Don't grow just the ordinary pale green sage; try deep purple or green-and-white-leaved varieties as well. They are lovely in the garden and in flower arrangements, and all are equally tasty. Bay is susceptible to frost, so gardeners in cold climates can grow it in a pot and bring it indoors in winter.

Thymes, marjoram, and oreganos have a host of uses in the kitchen, especially for Spanish and Italian recipes. Golden oregano and the very flavorful Greek oregano are worthy of places in any herb garden. The range of thymes alone could fill an entire garden bed, though the common green-leaved thyme remains the best for cooking. Lemon thyme has a pleasant tang. Most of us could not make spaghetti sauce without oregano, and it can also season chicken, beef, beans, eggplant, and more. Rosemary is an aromatic complement to lamb, pork, and chicken, but it is not hardy in the North. Cold-climate gardeners can grow rosemary in a pot and bring it indoors for winter.

Mints have a multitude of uses, but they are very vigorous growers that will take over the garden if given half a chance. Grow mints in pots, or with their roots contained, preferably away from other plants or sunk inside an old metal bucket or

GROW TRUE TARRAGON

True French tarragon cannot be grown from seed. If you see tarragon seeds for sale, don't buy them. Avoid Russian tarragon; it is not true tarragon and doesn't compare for flavor.

ROSEMARY AND LAVENDER

Rosemary and lavender cuttings often root if planted directly into the soil. Just snip off a healthy piece of stem just below a pair of leaves, strip off the leaves, and pop the cutting into the ground in a sheltered place, watering lightly.

Bay trees can be grown in pots and can be trimmed into decorative shapes.

Perennial Herb Varieties

Gardeners in the North can grow warm-climate herbs in pots and bring them indoors over winter.

Aloe vera (*Aloe barbadensis*)	Lemon verbena (*Aloysia triphylla*), warm climates
Anise hyssop (*Agastache foeniculum*)	Apple mint (*Mentha suaveolens*)
Bay (*Laurus nobilis*), warm climates	Orange mint (*Mentha* x *piperita* var. *citrata*)
Beebalm (*Monarda didyma*)	Peppermint (*Mentha* x *piperita*)
Roman chamomile (*Chamaemelum nobile*)	Spearmint (*Mentha spicata*)
Chives (*Allium sativum*)	Oregano (*Origanum vulgare*)
Fennel (*Foeniculum vulgare*)	Rosemary (*Rosmarinus officinalis*)
English lavender (*Lavandula angustifolia*)	Sage (*Salvia officinalis*)
French lavender (*Lavandula dentata*)	Tarragon (*Artemisia dracunculus*)
Lemongrass (*Cymbopogon citratus*), warm climates	Thyme (*Thymus* spp.)

a similar planter, or you will end up with mint rampaging through your garden. Try apple, ginger, and pineapple mint to flavor drinks as well as food. Lemon balm, another member of the mint clan, is equally thuggish, but it is delicious for herb teas and its delicate scent. Grow these plants near the edge of the path, where you will brush past them regularly and get full benefit of their fragrance.

Growing Perennial Herbs Mints are perennial and will grow in practically any soil, though they especially like one that's moist and humusy. Chives are not too fussy either, and lovage and horseradish also like deep, rich, damp soil and grow happily in shade. Most other herbs need warmth, prefer light, sandy soil, and need good drainage. Few Mediterranean herbs will survive sitting with wet feet in winter and some won't cope with frost. When choosing lavenders be particularly careful; Hidcote, Munstead and Folgate are hardy to Zone 5 but others need to be grown in pots and brought under cover to overwinter in cold areas.

Rosemary can also be variable. Where it is hardy it may thrive for years in a sunny site with well-drained soil, then one year it may get badly frost damaged and die back. So make sure you take cuttings regularly in case this happens. French tarragon is an excellent kitchen herb, but it needs protection in cool climates. You can take cuttings and protect them over winter.

Plant mints, lemon balm, and tansy in containers or into an old bucket in the soil to keep them from spreading too viciously.

Fresh basil is best known for its use in the Italian sauce, pesto.

Annual Herbs

Annual herbs need warmth and grow best in light soils in sunny beds or in pots on a sunny windowsill. Basil is a vital herb for the kitchen, and it is versatile, too. There are many different forms, including large- and small-leaved, purple- and green-leaved forms, aniseed basil, and Thai basil. Give basil a sunny spot in your garden or grow it in a pot on a sunny deck or patio. Small-leaved Greek basil is hardiest for outdoor growing, and it forms attractive little bushes that keep on producing for ages as you pick.

If you use cilantro often in cooking (it is important to Chinese and other Asian, as well as Mexican, cuisines), sow the seeds in rows in your vegetable patch if you have space. It grows and goes to flower and seed quickly, so you'll need to sow it regularly through the summer to keep a constant supply of greens and seeds to store.

Parsley belongs in every garden. Though it is a biennial, when plants bloom the foliage quality declines, so start with new plants every year. Flat-leaved, or Italian, parsley is easier to grow than the curly leaved type, and many cooks think it has better flavor.

Dill should be sown each year to ensure a good crop, although it may self-seed and crop up in unexpected spots in the garden. To prolong the harvest of leaves, clip off flowers as they form. Eventually the plants will bloom anyway, but you can then collect the seeds.

Saving Seeds If you want to save the seeds of dill, anise, caraway, cilantro, and other annual or biennial herbs, cut the stems when the seeds are ripe. Timing is everything; if you wait too long the seeds will fall to the ground and most will be lost. Watch the flowerheads as the seeds are maturing; when you see the seedpods just beginning to open, cut the stems. Place the stems in paper bags with the seed heads downward, and tie the bags shut. Place each herb in its own bag, and label all the bags. Hang the bags in a dry, airy place (an attic is often a good spot) and check them every day or two. When the seeds have fallen

GERMINATION JUMP START

To help parsley seeds germinate, pour a kettleful of boiling water over the seed drill to warm the soil right before you sow.

Rosemary is a popular addition to roast meat and potatoes.

A Dozen Annual Herbs

Anise (*Pimpinella anisum*)	German chamomile (*Matricaria recutita*)
Basil (*Ocimum basilicum*)	Marjoram (*Origanum majorana*), perennial in warm climates
Chervil (*Anthriscus cerefolium*)	Mexican marigold mint (*Tagetes lucida*)
Cilantro, coriander (*Coriandrum sativum*)	Parsley (*Petroselinum crispum*)
Cumin (*Cuminum cymium*)	Pineapple sage (*Salvia elegans*)
Dill (*Anethum graveolens*)	Summer savory (*Satureja hortensis*)

to the bottom of the bag, remove them and store in screw-top glass jars.

Knot Gardens

A knot garden is a traditional herb-hedged area—much loved in England since Tudor times and later popular in formal American gardens. It consists of low, clipped hedges of different herbs interwoven to make intricate patterns, sometimes with spaces between the hedges for planting. In other cases, the hedges make up the whole feature. Celtic knots are popular, but many formal designs work well. The design is created by weaving together different colored and textured herbs. Knot gardens make stunning features, but they require plenty of maintenance to keep them looking good.

A knot garden must be trimmed regularly to keep its intricate shape. Keep a simple design that will look striking but is relatively easy to maintain.

Knot Gardens Herbs

Dwarf boxwood (*Buxus microphylla*)
Germander (*Teucrium chamaedrys*)
Green santolina (*Santolina virens*)
Hyssop (*Hyssopus officinalis*)
Lavender (*Lavandula angustifolia*)
Lavender cotton (*Santolina chamaecyparissus*)
Wormwood (*Artemisia* spp.)

Different Types of Basil

There are many types of basil, used in cooking, decoration, and medicines, and for worship in some cultures.

Lemon basil is originally from northwest Africa and southern Asia.

Thai basil is most often found in Thai cuisine, but it is also popular in the United States.

Purple ruffles basil has won awards for its beauty and is easy to cultivate.

Spice basil grows in a bush form and has a very strong flavor.

Sweet basil is the most common variety, and it is often used to make Italian pesto.

HOMEMADE HERB TEA

For an instant healthy refreshment, make your own herb tea. Pick a handful of fresh lemon balm, mint leaves, or chamomile flowers, pour boiling water over the herbs, and let them steep for 5 minutes. Then strain and serve.

CARING FOR YOUR GARDEN

P lants are resilient. They will do their best to grow and reproduce in any conditions, but they do need attention—some more than others. The most important thing you can give your plants is a bit of your time. Get to know them; visit them regularly in your garden so you will notice when they look healthy or if they seem under the weather. Try to keep them as weed free as you can. You'll gradually learn how to recognize what different plants need and when.

As you get more involved in gardening you'll enjoy discovering how to keep the plants in tip-top shape and the joy of propagation—making make more plants without heading off to the garden center. Don't be alarmed when you see insects in your flowers or fruit and vegetables. Some are considered harmful, but others are actually beneficial to your garden. Ladybugs and stink bugs, for example, will eat harmful pests that attack your plants. Over time you'll learn which garden guests are welcome, and which are considered foes.

PROVIDING THE RIGHT CONDITIONS

Much of your job as a gardener is to provide the right conditions for your plants to thrive. In addition to giving them the amount of sun and type of soil that suits them best, you will need to pull weeds, water when the weather is dry, provide sufficient nutrients, and watch out for pests and diseases. Perennial flowers need to be divided periodically to remain vigorous. And trees and shrubs sometimes need pruning. However, the first step is planting and for many plants that begins with sowing seeds.

...to plant seeds, and watch the renewal of life—this is the commonest delight of the race, the most satisfactory thing a man can do.

—Charles Dudley Warner

The key to successful gardening is to understand the conditions your plants need to grow, and the conditions you have available on your property. Next put the plants in a place where you can give them what they need.

SOWING SEEDS INDOORS

Most annuals, many vegetables, and a lot of perennials are reasonably easy to grow from seed. A greenhouse is a wonderful thing to have if you enjoy sowing seeds, but a few sunny windowsills or some fluorescent lights are all you really need to get started. You can get dozens of tiny seedlings out of one seed tray.

You don't need much equipment to be an expert seed sower, and you can get most of it for free. The one thing you will need to buy is seed sowing mix or the ingredients to make your own. A planting mix for seeds needs to be lightweight and drain well. Many are based on peat and contain no soil. A soilless mix doesn't contain long-term nutrition, but your seeds and seedlings won't

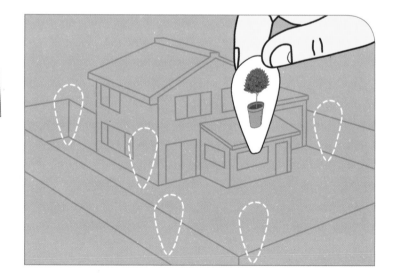

live in it for long. You can buy or make flats in which to start your seeds, or you can use small pots, peat pots, or recycled containers—old plastic tubs, yogurt cups, plastic takeout trays, or even pizza boxes can all be used as seed trays. Poke small drainage holes in the bottom of each container so excess water can drip out.

It is important to label your seed containers when you sow them—mark the name of the seed and the date you sow it. White plastic plant labels can be cleaned and reused very easily or use felt-tip marker on pieces of wood or wooden craft sticks. It is all too easy to forget to label things at the time of sowing and then move on to the next job, only to end up weeks later with crowds of hard-to-identify seedlings.

Fill your seed trays with planting mix, firm it down, and water well before sowing. Let the water soak the planting mix thoroughly, then let the excess drain off—you don't want to sow into puddles. Then follow the sowing instructions on the seed packet. It's hard to sow tiny seeds (such as those of begonias or petunias) evenly so you may want to mix them with fine sand, then put them in the palm of your hand, and close your hand around them. Let them dribble slowly out along the central line on your hand and try not to sow them in dense clumps. Larger seeds, such as those of nasturtiums, marigolds, and cornflowers, can be individually placed into the planting mix.

It's best to start your seeds out of direct sunlight or emerging seeds can get too hot and fry. To keep humidity high, cover seed trays with plastic until the seeds germinate—this keeps the seeds self-watered from water dripping off the plastic covering. You can uncover them and move them into a sunnier spot when seeds have germinated. The most important trick to raising seeds is to keep the planting mix evenly moist—do not let it dry out or get sodden.

Growing Seedlings Under Lights

A great way to provide seedlings with continuous, even light indoors is to set up one or more two-tube fluorescent light fixtures in your growing area. Use full-spectrum fluorescent lamps or a combination

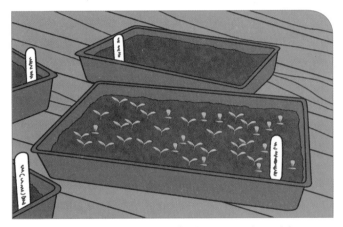

Sprinkle seeds evenly and thinly over the surface of the compost, leaving approximately ½–1 inch (1.2–2.5 cm) between each one. Cover seeds with a thin layer of compost.

Your seedlings should stay in a tray for about six weeks, and then you can pot them individually.

SIMPLE SEED VIABILITY TEST

To test the viability of seed you have stored from last year, drop the seeds into a bowl of water. Good seeds will sink and bad ones will float. Throw away the floaters and plant the rest. This test won't always work with very tiny seeds.

One for the rook, one
for the crow,
One to die and one
to grow,
Plant your seeds
in a row,
One for the pheasant,
one for the crow,
One to eat and
one to grow.

of cool white and warm white. The lights need to be just a few inches above the plant tops to provide enough light. You can either mount the light fixtures on chains, which you can gradually raise as the plants grow taller, or you can set the containers of seedlings atop stacks of books or bricks, which you can gradually lower as the plants grow. Keep the lights turned on for 12 to 15 hours a day.

Growing on Windowsills

If you're growing on windowsills, turn the seed trays regularly after seeds germinate to give the seedlings light on all sides. Otherwise they will get leggy and distorted, because they will grow toward the light.

SOWING SEEDS OUTDOORS

Many vegetables and hardy annual flowers get off to a good start when sown directly in the soil. When direct-sowing, two points are important to keep in mind: the temperature of the soil and its condition. However tempting it is to sow seeds on a bright, sunny day in early spring, try to resist. The soil will be too cold and probably too damp, and there will be more cold, wet weather to come. The seeds will probably rot in the ground and your seeds—and effort—will be wasted.

Also avoid sowing before you have cleared the seed bed as much as possible. Seeds cannot compete with more developed weed growth, and they will find it hard to compete with emerging weed seeds, which are often stronger and more determined to succeed. The ideal home for seeds is a beautifully cultivated and finely raked bed of loamy soil. Aim for that goal, but if you fall a bit short, don't worry. Seeds want to germinate and grow; it's their mission and they will do their best to fulfill it.

It's easiest to sow seeds in straight lines, and this is common practice in vegetable gardens, but you may wish to sow flower seed in patches or blocks. In places where you are growing vegetables or flowers as a cutting crop, draw a line to mark out seed drills, using short sections of bamboo canes or a length of string tied to two sticks. You can then easily weed between rows by hoeing as the seedlings grow. And when they have become strong enough, you can transplant them to their final destinations or leave them in rows, if you like.

Sow seeds in straight lines and well spaced. You can thin out fine seeds later if you sowed them too thickly.

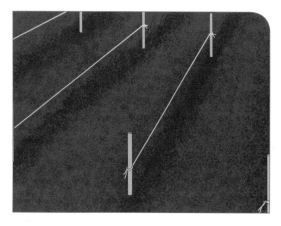

Preparing Soil for Seeding

To get healthy and predictable results from your seeds, prepare the soil before you sow. You'll need to start the process two to three weeks beforehand, allowing weeds to germinate. Once you've removed the offending plants, your seeds won't have to compete for water, light, and space.

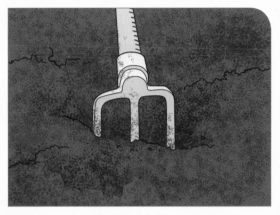

1 Cultivate the soil to be ready for sowing.

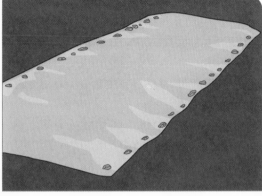

2 Cover with floating row covers or plastic.

3 After two weeks, remove the covering; weed seedlings will have germinated.

4 Hoe off weed seedlings, leaving the ground clear for sowing.

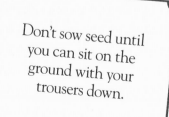

Don't sow seed until you can sit on the ground with your trousers down.

A GOOD START FOR TINY SEEDS

To improve germination of tiny seeds, press them lightly into moist soil but do not cover them. Sprinkle finely sieved compost, sand, or milled sphagnum moss on top of them. Water by misting them.

Butterflies help your garden by assisting pollination.

Keep an eye on germinating seeds and seedlings in the ground. They need to be kept moist, just like indoor sowings, and you also need to watch out for the many pests that can decimate young plants. Slugs are major culprits, so take measures to keep them at bay.

CARING FOR SEEDLINGS

As seeds that were started indoors germinate and grow into seedlings, the trays soon become overcrowded. Once outdoors, the young plants jostle for space in rows in the ground. This is when seedlings need to be thinned and transplanted into roomier accommodations; otherwise none of them will have the chance to grow successfully. Conventional wisdom says you need to thin out when a seedling has three strong leaves, but it doesn't matter if you leave it a bit longer. Be careful separating the seedlings, always pick them up by the leaves, not the stem, or you may damage the important cells that transport nutrients through the plant.

Separate seedlings with a small, plastic plant label or thin pencil, and support the root end on the label as you move them into new potting mix or a new spot in the ground. You need something to make holes in the soil or compost. You can buy a custom-made dibble, but the end of a pencil, a pointy stick, or a spoon handle all work fine.

Transplant indoor-grown seedlings into plastic pots or similar containers in late spring, or if you've made later sowings, transplant them straight into the ground in summer. Remember all seedlings are very delicate and need to be protected from rough weather and given plenty of warmth, moisture, and light. Outdoor seedlings are much tougher than their indoor cousins, but they still need attention when you first thin and move them. Newly transplanted seedlings may wilt and sulk for the first couple of days before perking up and getting on with life.

When transplanting seedlings from indoors to the garden, be sure they can tolerate outdoor weather conditions. Tender plants, such as tomatoes and impatiens, cannot withstand frost or cold temperatures. Even cold-tolerant seedlings need to be hardened off to make an easier transition to outdoor life. Also check recommended spacing distances for your plants, and place them accordingly when you transplant them into the garden.

To transplant, carefully dig up small plants using a butter knife or wooden plant label. Pick plants out one at a time.

Hardening Off Seedlings

Acclimatize seedlings to outdoor conditions before you transplant them outdoors. Place their containers in a sheltered outdoor location, such as a porch or an open cold frame. The first day, leave the seedlings outdoors for two to three hours, then move them back inside. Over the next six or seven days, leave the seedlings outdoors for a longer time each day, until you are able to leave them outside overnight. Then they are ready to transplant. If the weather turns unseasonably cold or stormy, wait until conditions moderate to transplant the seedlings.

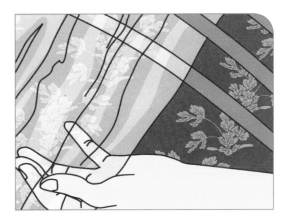

Protection is important for newly transplanted seedlings. One way to protect them from the elements is with plastic sheeting draped over wooden supports. This serves as a makeshift greenhouse.

INCREASING PLANTS BY DIVISION AND LAYERING

The easiest way to increase your stock of herbaceous perennials is to divide existing ones. Most perennials need to be divided from time to time to maintain their vigor, some more often than others. To divide a plant you need to dig it up or use a sharp spade to split a large clump into smaller pieces, then dig up the sections you want to move. Replant the pieces and you'll have a mass of new plants for free. Not only will you get a stock of new plants, you will be doing the original plant a favor—many perennials like to be split every three or four years to keep them vigorous and healthy.

DIVIDING IN CLAY SOIL

If you garden in heavy clay, wait until spring before dividing, because plants risk getting waterlogged in winter and young plants might not survive.

Perennials That Seldom Need Division

These perennials can go for years without being divided:

Aconitum spp., monkshood	*Geranium* spp., cranesbill
Aruncus dioicus, goatsbeard	*Gypsophila paniculata*, baby's breath
Asclepias tuberosa, butterfly weed	*Helleborus* spp., hellebores
Baptisia australis, blue false indigo	*Hemerocallis* spp., daylily
Brunnera macrophylla, Siberian bugloss	*Hosta* spp., plantain lily
Chelone spp., turtlehead	*Iris sibirica*, Siberian iris
Cimicifuga racemosa, black snakeroot	*Paeonia* spp., peony
Dicentra spp., bleeding heart	*Papaver orientale*, Oriental poppy
Dictamnus albus, gas plant	*Platycodon grandiflorus*, balloon flower
Epimedium spp., barrenwort	*Veronica* spp., speedwell

Splitting Plants with Large Clumped Roots

Split plants with fleshy roots, such as hostas and daylilies, with a sharp knife. Lift the plants and rinse excess soil from the roots so you can see new growth buds clearly, then use a sharp knife to take off sections with lots of buds and roots and replant them.

1 Place two forks back to back in clump of plants, such as Michaelmas daisies (asters).

2 Move the forks to tease the clump apart.

It is best to divide plants when they are semidormant and the ground is easily workable—in fall or spring. The general rule is that perennials that flower in the first half of summer need to be divided in fall, while late-summer or fall bloomers aren't divided until spring. Split them just as new growth is beginning to get going.

Each new piece of plant must be complete with roots and growth buds—which are found on the crown, where stems meet roots. Plant the new sections directly into their final homes. Firm new plants into the ground with your hands or feet and water them in well. They may droop for a few days but will be looking content within a week. Keep the soil evenly moist—not soggy—for several weeks as the plants settle in and begin to send new roots out into the soil.

Divide plants with large clumps of tough, fibrous roots, such as hardy geraniums, asters, and Siberian iris, by digging up the clump you want to split and plunging two forks back to back through the center of the plant. Just push and pull the two forks apart to split the clump into sections—you might need a helper. You can also use a sharp spade to divide the root clump. If a clump gets really large with very tightly congested roots, you may need to hack at it with a saw or even a hatchet or machete. Don't worry, the plant will love you for it in the long run. At the other extreme, clumps of primroses can be simply teased apart with your hands.

TIME TO DIVIDE

How do you know when it is time to divide a plant? One signal is when it seems to lose its vigor and no longer grows and blooms as well as it used to. If you notice that the center of a clump of stems seems empty, with the plant appearing to grow in a ring around it, the plant is in desperate need of division.

Ivy can easily be propagated using the layering method.

Layering

The easiest method to increase woody plants and climbers is to simply peg a shoot of an existing plant into the ground and wait for it to take root. Then sever your rooted section from the parent plant and replant it. Herbs, such as sage and thyme, will root where they touch the ground; other plants need a little help. The best time to layer many plants is in early spring, as soon as the soil can be worked.

1 Choose a flexible, healthy shoot that can be bent to touch the ground.

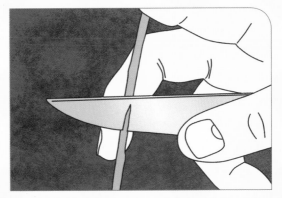

2 While holding the shoot in one hand and a sharp knife in the other, carefully make a cut in the underside of the stem, without cutting it all the way through.

3 Pin the shoot into the ground with a metal peg.

4 Dig up the rooted section in a few months and sever it from the parent.

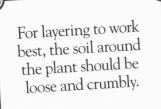

For layering to work best, the soil around the plant should be loose and crumbly.

PROPAGATE BY LAYERING

Plants that respond well to layering have long, flexible stems.

Plants to Propagate by Layering

Clematis spp.	*Hibiscus* spp.
Cotoneaster spp.	*Hydrangea petiolaris*, climbing hydrangea
Dianthus spp., garden pinks	*Jasminum* spp., jasmine
Forsythia spp.	*Lonicera* spp., honeysuckle
Fragaria spp., strawberries	*Parthenocissus* spp., Boston ivy, Virginia creeper
Hamamelis spp., witch hazel	*Rubus* spp., raspberries and blackberries
Hedera spp., ivy	*Vitis* spp., grapes

PLANTING CUTTINGS ROOTED IN WATER

For a gentle transition when it's time to plant cuttings that have rooted in water, add soil to the water gradually over a few weeks, so the roots can adapt to the new environment.

Make your own rooting hormone compound. Boil a few chopped up willow stems in water for 10 minutes and leave the liquid to cool, then dip the ends of your cuttings into this before planting them. Willow contains salicylates that help plants root.

INCREASING PLANTS BY CUTTINGS

Most shrubs and plants with woody stems are propagated by taking cuttings from their stems, and you can also increase many perennials through stem tip cuttings. Amateur gardeners are often frightened of taking cuttings—it sounds as though it should be left to the professionals. But it is genuinely easy to take cuttings. You may not succeed with all of them, but it costs no more than a container of potting mix to give it a try.

Stem, Tip, and Softwood Cuttings

Most cuttings are taken from the stems of plants, but you can also take them from leaves or roots. Some plants are so desperate to root that you only need to put their cuttings in a jar of water and they're off. Mints, catmint, coleus, penstemons, ivy, mophead or bigleaf hydrangeas, and begonias will all root this way. Just take a stem, cut off the lower leaves and make a clean cut with a sharp knife before putting the stem in a jar of water. Keep the water level topped up to keep the stems submerged and wait two to six weeks. To keep the stems upright, place a piece of chicken wire over the top of the jar, secure it around the rim with a rubber band or string, and put your stems through this support. Once roots appear, pot young plants into good potting mix, and keep them well watered until they get established.

Stem, tip, or softwood cuttings are usually taken from the soft stem tip growth of this season's growth, when plants are about midway through the growing season. Look for stems that are neither very young and soft, nor old and woody. Chrysanthemums, lavenders, and other herbs root speedily from softwood cuttings.

Tip Cutting

Dip the cutting tool in rubbing alcohol or a mixture of one part bleach to nine parts water. This prevents you from transmitting diseases from any infected plants to healthy ones. Always use a very sharp knife to avoid harming your parent plant unnecessarily.

1 Cut a strong young shoot from the parent plant, up to 8 inches (20 cm) long, cutting just below a node or pair of leaves. This is where the plant's hormones are concentrated.

2 Remove the lower leaves so that half the stem is clear.

3 Fill a pot with potting mix and insert the stem of your cutting. Some gardeners like to dip the end of the stem into rooting hormone powder first—especially for cuttings from shrubs or woody vines—but it's not absolutely necessary.

4 Water and cover the pot and cutting with a clear plastic bag to keep moisture inside. Keep the cutting in the shade, and check it periodically to be sure the soil does not dry out. Open the bag to let in fresh air.

Plants to Propagate from Cuttings

Artemisia spp.	*Gaillardia* spp., blanketflower
Ascelpias tuberosa, butterfly weed	*Hydrangea* spp. (except for *H. quercifolia*)
Begonia semperflorens, wax begonia	*Ilex verticillata*, winterberry
Buddleia spp., butterfly bush	*Lavandula* spp., lavender
Camellia spp.	*Pelargonium* cvs., geranium
Campanula spp., bellflower	*Rhododendron* spp., deciduous azaleas
Clethra alnifolia, summersweet	*Rosa* spp., species roses
Cornus spp., dogwood	*Sedum spectabile*, showy stonecrop
Dendrathema cvs., chrysanthemum	*Spiraea* spp., spirea
Dianthus spp., garden pinks	*Viburnum* spp.

Heel Cuttings

Heel, or semiripe, cuttings are also taken from the current season's growth, with a bit of woody tissue from the main stem attached at the base. Take heel cuttings in mid- to late summer, when the new growth is beginning to harden. The process is otherwise the same as for stem tip cuttings, but they take longer to root.

Butterfly bush, fuchsia, hydrangeas, rock rose (*Cistus* spp.), and honeysuckle are suitable candidates.

Hardwood Cuttings

At planting time, prepare a cuttings bed in good soil in a semishaded part of the garden and make holes about 6 inches (15 cm) deep for the cuttings. Sprinkle horticultural sand into the base of each hole and insert the cuttings. Water and firm them in well. They will stay in the cuttings bed for a year before they can be moved and need protection from heavy frosts.

Heel cuttings should be taken from only nonflowering, healthy side shoots that are soft at the top and just starting to harden at the base.

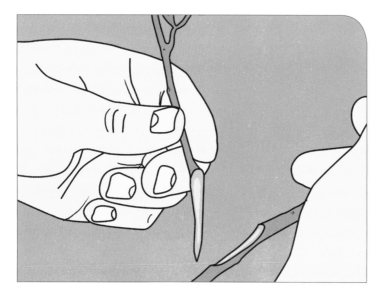

Taking Hardwood Cuttings

Hardwood cuttings are taken from the mature woody stems of this season's growth, when the plant is dormant and the year's growth has hardened. The best time is in fall, after deciduous trees and shrubs have dropped their leaves. Take cuttings from the ends of healthy branches that have grown from the base of the plant. Don't use spindly or late-season stems.

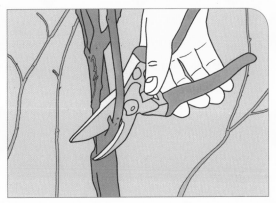

1 Take a healthy shoot about 12 inches (30 cm) long, cutting it straight across the stem just below a bud.

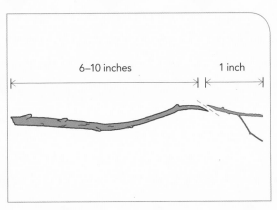

2 Remove the top inch (2.5 cm) of the stem, cut the tip on an angle, and cut the stem into pieces 6–10 inches (15–25 cm) long.

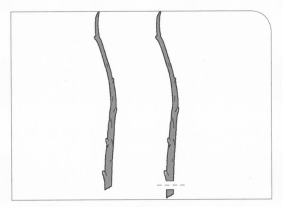

3 Cut the bottom straight and the top on an angle, so you will be able to tell the top from bottom when planting the cuttings. Each cutting should have at least three nodes (dormant buds).

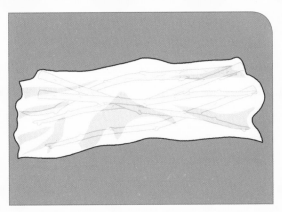

4 Cover the cuttings with a damp cloth as you prepare them, so they don't dry out.

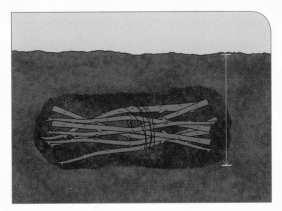

5 Dip the bottom of each cutting in rooting hormone powder or willow water before planting. In colder climates, bundle the cuttings and store them in a 12-inch (30-cm) deep trench in the garden or cold frame and plant them in spring. In much milder climates, plant cuttings right away.

Root Cuttings

Root cuttings need reasonable compost, a moderate but steady temperature, space, and a little patience. Plants with fleshy roots, such as Oriental poppies (*Papaver orientale*), can be increased from root cuttings.

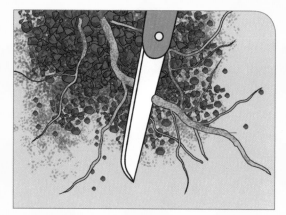

1 Dig up the plant when it is dormant, cut off one or two thick roots then return the parent plant to its place.

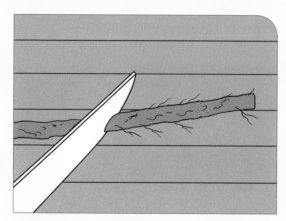

2 With a sharp knife, cut the roots into sections about 2–3 inches (5–7.5 cm) long.

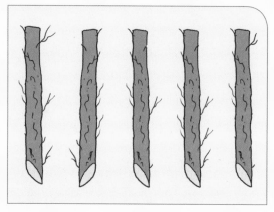

3 Slice them straight at the top and angle them at the base.

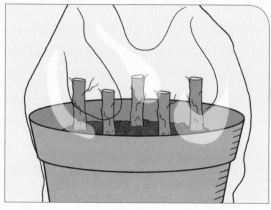

4 Insert cuttings into a pot of moist potting mix containing some sand. Keep the medium moist and the cuttings should sprout within six months.

PRUNING

Plants need to be pruned, which simply means they need to be cut back from time to time. There is an art to pruning, but it's something you learn by practicing. The good news is that you can hardly ever kill anything by overpruning it, so if you make a bit of a slip with your pruners, loppers, or knife it probably won't really matter.

The first job when pruning is to remove any dead, dying, or diseased material, then take out any woody stems or branches that are crossing and rubbing against each other. The final stage is pruning for shape.

Deadheading Perennials

Perennials simply need deadheading to encourage more flowers to form during their flowering season, and you can chop spent flower stalks of lupines, delphiniums, and many tall species to the ground to encourage another flush of flowers.

Pruning Shrubs

While some shrubs are happy with little more than an occasional light trim to keep them happy, others need regular pruning so they continue to grow and flower well.

When to Prune Prune shrubs that flower in spring, such as forsythias, lilacs, azaleas, rhododendrons, flowering quince, and deutzia, after they finish blooming. These shrubs flower on wood produced the previous year, and set next year's flower buds after this year's flowers finish blooming. If you wait until fall or spring to prune, you risk cutting off the flowers-to-be.

Shrubs that flower later in the year, such as summersweet, caryopteris, and beautyberry, bloom on new wood and can be pruned while dormant, in winter or early spring. Hydrangeas are a special case. Of course, there are exceptions to every rule. Find out the right time to prune each shrub in your landscape.

DON'T PRUNE IN FALL

One important thing to remember is never to prune plants just before winter. For example, if you give your lavender a severe haircut late in October, it will respond by sending out masses of new shoots that won't have a chance to harden off before cold frosty weather, and it will likely suffer winterkill.

Keep your pruning tools clean and sharp so you don't damage the plant and put it at risk of disease or pests attacking weak spots.

DON'T PRUNE FOR SIZE

To avoid unnecessary pruning, choose a tree or shrub that when fully mature will fit the space you have available for it.

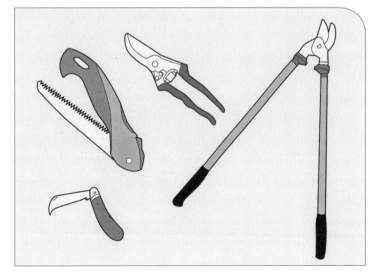

Pruning Deciduous Shrubs

These shrubs lose their leaves in winter and renew themselves in the spring, so prune annually.

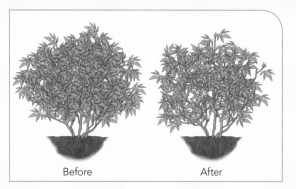

Before   After

1 Remove up to one third of the stems from a congested plant to provide air flow.

2 Cut out any thin, weak, distorted, or spindly stems.

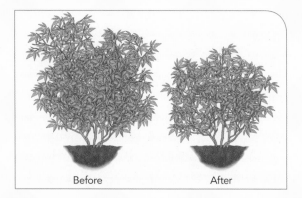

Before   After

3 Cut back overvigorous shoots that spoil the balance, but don't cut these back hard or you'll end up with more vigorous growth.

Pruning Hydrangeas

Hydrangea pruning is confusing to many gardeners. When to prune depends on whether the plants bloom on new or old wood.

Mophead and lacecap varieties (*Hydrangea macrophylla*) and oakleaf hydrangea (*H. quercifolia*) bloom on old wood. Deadhead the flowers in fall or spring. It is best to do no other pruning and let the plants assume their natural forms. But if you need to prune because the plant has grown straggly or too big for its space, do it as soon as the flowers fade, cutting back to the fat flower buds on the stem. Some newer macrophylla varieties, such as Endless Summer, bloom on both old and new wood, so whenever you prune you should still get some flowers next summer.

Panicle or peegee hydrangea (*Hydrangea paniculata*) and smooth-leaved hydrangea (*H. arborescens*), the best-known of which is Annabelle, bloom on new growth and may be pruned anytime from fall to spring. Cut peegee back to leave two or three buds on each stem. Cut Annabelle back to the ground.

Pruning Trees

Follow a few basic principles and you won't go wrong with tree pruning. But if you have an orchard or mini-arboretum and need to prune lots of trees, it would be wise to equip yourself with a detailed tree-pruning manual.

Most deciduous trees are best pruned when dormant, in winter or very early spring. The exceptions to the "deciduous tree" rule include

SIGNAL TO PRUNE

When a shrub needs pruning, it will get straggly and produce flowers and foliage unevenly over the bush. Some unpruned shrubs end up with all the new growth at the top and unsightly bare branches elsewhere.

When to Prune Shrubs

Little or no pruning required	
Abelia x *grandiflora*, glossy abelia	*Cornus sericea*, red-osier dogwood
Amelanchier spp., serviceberry	*Cotinus coggygria*, smokebush
Buddleia globosa, orange butterfly bush (warm climates)	*Forsythia* x *intermedia*
Deutzia gracilis 'Nikko', slender deutzia	*Hydrangea paniculata, H. arborescens*, peegee hydrangea, smooth-leaved hydrangea
Hamamelis spp., witch hazel	*Lavandula* spp., lavender
Hibiscus syriacus, rose-of-Sharon	*Salvia officinalis*, sage
Hydrangea quercifolia, oakleaf hydrangea	
Kalmia latifolia, mountain laurel	**Prune in summer**
Osmanthus x *fortunei*, Fortune's osmanthus (warm climates)	*Buddleia alternifolia*, fountain buddleia
Pieris japonica, Japanese pieris	*Chaenomeles* spp., flowering quince
Pittosporum tobira, Japanese pittosporum (warm climates)	*Cytisus scoparius*, Scotch broom
	Deutzia spp.
Rhododendron spp., azalea and rhododendron	*Exochorda racemosa*, pearlbush
Viburnum spp.	*Hydrangea macrophylla, H. quercifolia*, bigleaf hydrangea, oakleaf hydrangea
	Kerria japonica, Japanese kerria
Prune in spring	*Kolkwitzia amabilis*, beautybush
Abeliophyllum distichum, Korean forsythia	*Philadelphus coronarius*, mock orange
Buddleia davidii, butterfly bush	*Spiraea japonica*, Japanese spirea
Caryopteris x *clandonensis*, blue-mist shrub	*Weigela florida*, old-fashioned weigela

Pruning Alternately Arranged Shrubs

The leaves on these shrubs alternate direction along the stem, so prune carefully to avoid taking off too much.

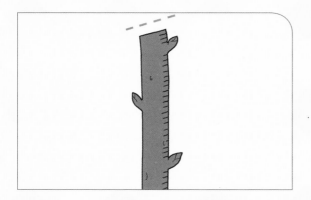

1 On plants with buds arranged alternately down the stem, prune with an angled cut just above an outward facing bud. A new shoot will then grow away from the main stem.

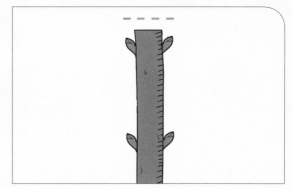

2 On plants with pairs of buds opposite each other on the stem, prune with a straight cut just above a pair of buds.

birch, cherry, elm, horse chestnut, and walnut trees, which all bleed extensively, even toward the end of their dormant season. Prune them in midsummer after new growth has matured.

Conifers require little or no regular pruning except the removal of dead or diseased branches. This bad growth needs to be removed anytime you see it.

The shapes and forms of trees vary, but the two main types are trees with a dominant vertical central branch, or leader, and multibranched trees. If you remove the central leader, this diverts the main growth hormones to lower branches and allows them to grow strongly. Think carefully before you intentionally remove an obvious leader on a very upright tree. Removing it will spoil the shape of the tree. If a leader is damaged, perhaps in a storm, then prune the damaged leader back to a healthy bud and train the shoot that emerges against a bamboo cane (supported in turn by a wooden splint, if necessary) so it grows vertically. Once the new leader becomes woody, you can remove the cane and the shoot will grow vertically without support.

Young deciduous trees need to be carefully pruned to develop a balanced framework with a straight stem and well-spaced branches. The first three years are the most important. After planting remove competing shoots and any that are thin or cross over. Also remove extra vertical branches that might form a double trunk (unless the tree is a clump-forming type, such as birch). The next year remove small branches that will compete with the main, or scaffold, branches, as well as those at a narrow angle to the trunk, and branches that could compete with the central leader.

Fruit trees must be pruned annually, but mature ornamental trees need to be pruned only to keep them in shape and healthy by thinning out crowded, crossing, or diseased or damaged branches. You may also need to reduce the size of large branches that spoil the balance of the tree.

Basic tree pruning

- Prune trees to remove dead, damaged, or diseased wood whenever you notice it.

- Remove watersprouts, which grow vertically from branches, as soon as you see them.

- Remove crossed or rubbing branches.

- Remove branches that meet the trunk at an angle less than 45 degrees.

Topiary

It's fun to cut trees or bushes into ornamental shapes, but you need patience, because it takes up to 10 years to create a good specimen from scratch, and you must choose the right variety of plant to be successful. You can also train vines over wire forms to create topiaries.

CREATING TOPIARY SHAPES

- **Globes** Trim a central circular band around the middle before tackling the top and bottom.
- **Cones (pyramids and obelisks)** Create straight "corners" and verticals before tackling the sides and horizontals. This will help prevent one-sidedness. Alternatively, place a wire form over the plant and only start clipping once the plant has grown through it. A form can be removed once the outline of the shape has developed.

- **Spirals** Train the main shoot to a central pole, shortening all lateral branches to 6 inches (10 cm) in early and late summer. When the plant reaches its desired height, start to clip the foliage to create the lowest coil of the spiral. This should be long and wide, the spirals tightening and shortening up the stem.
- **Irregular shapes** Follow a wire template, working from the top downward.

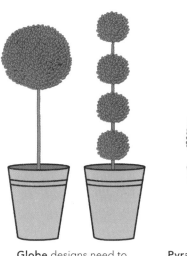

Globe designs need to be started in the middle.

Pyramid shapes start with trimming four corners.

Spiral shapes need to be trained to a pole.

Irregular shapes are made following templates.

Easiest Evergreens for Fine Topiary

Buxus spp., boxwood	Large-leaved evergreens, for bigger topiaries
Lavandula spp. Lavender	*Elaeagnus ebbingei* (for warm climates)
Lonicera nitida, evergreen honeysuckle	*Ilex* spp., hollies
Rosmarinus spp., rosemary	*Laurus nobilis*, bay
Taxus baccata, yew	*Prunus laurocerasus*, cherry laurel

Pruning Climbers

People get confused about when to prune climbers, but most are straightforward. The secret to getting the best display from climbers has as much to do with training as pruning. Train as much growth as possible on the horizontal rather than vertical. If stems are allowed to grow directly upward, they become bare at the base and you only get flowers high up. Horizontal training also encourages the growth of plenty of new sideshoots, so you get more flowers and foliage.

Roses The most difficult thing about pruning climbing roses is reaching particularly tall or thorny plants. Wear good protective clothing and heavy, long gloves when tackling them, and always have someone with you if the job requires climbing a ladder. Climbing roses should be pruned in late winter to keep the plants in check, to remove any damaged or spindly growth, and to promote better flowering. Prune when the buds begin to swell but plants are not yet growing actively. Rambler roses are more vigorous than climbers, and regular pruning keeps them flowering freely. Trim them back after flowering any time from late summer to early fall, and keep them in good shape by removing at ground level about a third of the older stems and taking out branches that are outgrowing their space. Fasten new vigorous shoots that will flower next year to supports, and shorten side shoots by about a third.

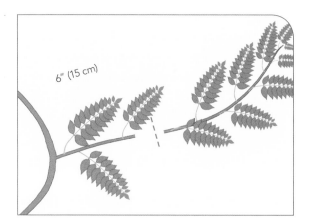

6" (15 cm)

Wisteria is a climbing vine, which sprouts beautiful flowers. These plants are loved by gardeners around the world.

Wisteria The simplest, most-effective method to be sure of a good show of blooms is to prune wisteria hard in summer after flowering, any time from late June to August. This encourages the development of short flowering spurs that will carry the flowers next spring. Cut all the long shoots that have been produced during the late spring and early summer back to about 6 inches (15 cm) from the main stems. In late winter, cut back these spurs to 3–4 inches (8–10 cm), leaving two or three buds at the base of the current season's growth.

Clematis Every garden should have at least one clematis; there are many different and beautiful forms, they're thorn free and easy to keep in check. But pruning them is confusing to many gardeners. There are three ways to prune clematis, depending on when they bloom.

Cultivars bred from *Clematis patens* and *Clematis florida* bloom on old growth. Cut back hard several of the oldest stems right after blooming, to promote new growth that will flower next year. Cultivars in this group include 'Bees Jubilee', 'Belle of Woking', 'Marcel Morse', and 'Duchess of Edinburgh'.

Some varieties bloom on old wood in late spring or early summer and may flower again on new growth later in the season. Prune them in late winter to early spring, before growth begins. Cut back stems to a strong pair of buds 2–4 feet (80–150 cm) off the ground. This group includes 'Elsa Spath', 'Fairy Queen', 'Henryi', and 'Nelly Moser'.

Clematis jackmanii and its hybrids flower on new growth, mostly in summer and early fall. Prune them in late winter to early spring, cutting back to the lowest set of good buds on each stem. For taller plants, cut back the stems to 4–6 inches (8–15 cm) above that pair of buds. This group includes 'Comtesse de Bouchard', 'Duchess of Albany', 'Ernest Markham', 'Hagley Hybrid', and 'Huldine'.

Prune clematis to just above a pair of healthy buds or single bud. Tie in unpruned growth horizontally where possible.

WATERING

Plants need water, and it's best to give it to them efficiently—in a way that will meet their needs, while not wasting water. Surprisingly, problems are more common from giving plants too much rather than too little water, because most plants adapt better to semidrought than to overwatering. Always water in the cool of the day, before the sun is high and just before it is going down, and try to water regularly to keep the soil or compost moist. You are setting up problems if you give plants a large amount one day, almost drown them the next, and then wait until they are all almost dry before watering again.

In a small garden you may need only a watering can, fitted with different rose attachments to allow different flow patterns—you need a fine rose for tender seedlings and a large one for established plants. A handheld hose is generally most useful, you can regulate the flow by using a spray nozzle on the end and direct water to the roots of plants where they need it most. Overhead sprinklers are popular but should only be used with caution. They can be very wasteful, because they water areas that may not need water as well as those that do. Plus the water hits the tops of plants and trickles to the ground rather than getting straight to the roots.

Ground-Level Watering

Less wasteful than overhead watering, ground level watering is more efficient and automatic—you don't have to be there to keep your plants watered. Few gardens need a complicated irrigation system, but inexpensive soaker hoses—hoses with tiny perforations or porous tubes that allow water to seep into the ground—are an efficient way of getting water right to the root zone of your plants. You simply lay the hoses between your plants and forget about watering. The disadvantage is that they are not beautiful, and they can clog with garden debris. Drip systems are more expensive. The porous pipes are generally buried just beneath the soil to deliver water to the plant roots, and they are effective, efficient, and save you work. Be sure to get the right size emitter for your soil type. You can put drip systems or soaker hoses on a timer to deliver the water at the time you prefer.

BEST TIMES FOR OVERHEAD SPRINKLING

If you water from overhead, never water in bright sunshine or you risk scorching leaves. Water in early morning or early evening. The leaves should dry before dark or the chance of disease increases.

Ways to Conserve Water

These simple methods can get you on your way to becoming an environmentally friendly gardener.

- Mulch the garden.
- Make a shallow depression in the soil around the base of each plant to catch and hold rainwater.
- Use a drip system or soaker hoses.
- Don't water during the hottest part of day, when more will be lost to evaporation.
- Build humusy soil that can hold water longer without becoming waterlogged.
- Save water in a rain barrel to use on plants.
- Water only when you need to, not automatically.
- Plant more for spring and fall, and less for summer.
- Plant in blocks instead of rows so you need to water over a smaller area.

NONCHEMICAL PEST CONTROL

You can't avoid pests in any garden; they are part of the ecosystem. But this doesn't mean you have to welcome them all and try to live together. Some pests cause havoc and must be kept under control.

Each year more pest controls fly onto the market, but some of the old-fashioned ways are still the best—and the cheapest. Companion planting is a good start (see page 133) and so is planting specifically to encourage beneficial insects. You can buy pheromone traps to catch yellowjackets and Japanese beetles, douse cabbages in rhubarb-leaf tea to stop them being decimated by caterpillars, or you can just pick bugs off your plants or wash them off with soapy water. You may come across biological controls, such as nematodes for slugs or BTK against caterpillars, but these are most effective in a fairly controlled environment and are not suitable for all gardens. Try other methods first.

Slugs and Snails

Slugs and snails are major garden pests. They seem to be everywhere in gardens where moisture is abundant, sucking young seedlings to death, nipping off tender growth, and turning precious foliage into hideous fretwork overnight. The best prevention is to spread around precious plants something gritty, such as lava rock or diatomaceous earth, which are sharp and pierce the pests' skins. But these materials can also harm some beneficial insects, so use them with caution.

If your garden is not too large, you can seduce slugs with their favorite drink. The trick is to lay beer traps for them to fall into. Partially bury saucers or jars of beer among your plants to act as magnets for slugs. Or lay upturned grapefruit halves and comfrey leaves on your beds to encourage slugs to congregate and remove them regularly. Slugs don't like crossing copper, so you can buy copper strips to surround your plants. Some gardeners find that spreading baked and crushed eggshells around the garden keeps slugs away, and others have great success with coffee grounds (try getting some from your local coffee shop). The best idea of all is to go out first thing in the morning and last thing in the evening and painstakingly pick up every slug and snail you see and squash them or desiccate them by covering them in salt.

PEST CONTROL

Don't put out chemical slug pellets unless you get desperate, because these are bad for the birds that eat snails and slugs. A good, effective alternative is iron phosphate slug bait, which causes no harm to plants, wildlife, or people.

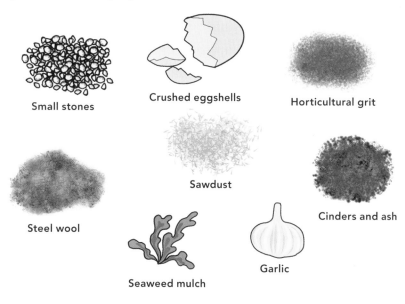

Small stones

Crushed eggshells

Horticultural grit

Steel wool

Sawdust

Seaweed mulch

Garlic

Cinders and ash

Antislug mulches are available in many varieties. Some are store-bought, and others can be made using simple household items.

PROTECTION FROM CUTWORMS

Cutworms are gray or dull brown caterpillars with shiny heads that live just below the surface of the soil and feed at night on the stems of seedlings and transplants, particularly in early summer. A cardboard collar pushed 2 inches (5 cm) into the soil around a young plant will protect it.

Aphids

Aphids are also high up on the list of vandals. The little sucking insects may be white, brown, green, or other colors, and you can find them clustered on stems, undersides of leaves, and in leaf axils. Fortunately they become less and less of a problem the more variety of plants you grow, because other insects will be attracted to specific plants and will also feed off aphids. Hoverflies, lacewings, and ladybugs are all highly beneficial in your garden—aphids are among their favorite foods. Encourage the good bugs to inhabit your garden by planting their favorite host plants—umbellifers, such as fennel and dill. In a few years, you won't have a problem.

APHID TRAPS

Paint small squares of heavy cardboard bright yellow, and coat the surface with oil or another sticky substance. Then hang the traps in the garden. Aphids and whiteflies will be attracted to the yellow cards and get stuck. When the cardboard is covered with bugs, toss it in the trash.

Making Rhubarb Leaf Tea

While it is not for drinking, this tea will keep bugs and pests away when sprayed onto your garden plants.

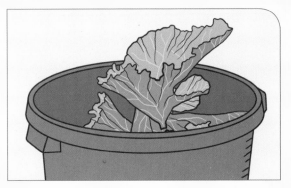

1 Collect at least eight large rhubarb leaves and place in a bucket or trash can.

2 Pour on 4 x 11 pint (2 x 5 liter) watering cans full of water and cover the bucket or trash can with a lid.

3 After two weeks you can use the liquid. Water brassicas when cabbage white butterflies are laying their eggs and when caterpillars are hatching.

Cabbage Butterflies

Vegetable gardeners hate the cabbage white butterfly; its caterpillars can munch through dozens of sprout and cabbage plants in a night. If cabbage worms and the resulting butterflies are a plague in your garden, try an old-fashioned remedy. Water your brassicas well with rhubarb leaf tea—nothing more than rhubarb leaves steeped in water. Dose your plants liberally with this and you may find that the butterflies stay away or their caterpillars die. Suddenly the plants don't seem so tasty any more.

Deer

Deer are a huge problem in some areas. The only foolproof way to keep them out is to enclose your garden in a 10-foot-high (3-m-high) fence. Try setting up some outdoor lights to come on and off at irregular intervals during the night (tell your neighbors first if this will affect their property, too).

Other strategies are to grow plants deer don't usually eat—though their appetites change and expand constantly—to repel them with barking dogs, devices that squirt water when stepped on or make loud noise, or hanging bags of human hair or deodorant soap. Spraying plants with natural repellents containing hot pepper, eggs, and other unpleasant materials is effective, but you'll need to switch among different repellents as the deer become used to them.

TRAP EARWIGS

Earwigs are notorious; they chew holes in leaves and flowers and collect inside heads of lettuce. To trap them crumple some newspaper and put it inside cardboard tubes from rolls of toilet tissue or paper towels. In the evening set the tubes in the garden and the earwigs will hide in them. In the morning empty the traps and crush the bugs.

RECOGNIZING AND TREATING DISEASES

Diseases generally strike weak or damaged plants or plants that are struggling in poor soil or the wrong soil conditions, so the best cure for plant ailments is usually to prevent them in the first place. A healthy garden where plants are well cared for should be fairly free from disease. Sometimes, though, wet weather and other environmental conditions allow viral or fungal disease organisms to take hold and cause problems.

Keep your tools clean, particularly pruning tools, because dirt can easily enter a new cut on a plant, which makes a weak spot for bacteria to enter. Practice good hygiene in the garden, too. Pull the weeds, pick up fallen leaves and other plant debris. If plants do get affected by disease, strip off affected leaves or stems and put them in the trash—never compost diseased plant material.

Monitor your garden for pests and disease. Keep a lookout for early signs of sickness. Yellowing and curling leaves are often signs that something is wrong, as are early leaf fall or blotches on stems and foliage. These might be due to lack of some nutrients in the soil, so it's often worth feeding the plant as a first resort if you do not see secondary symptoms of disease.

OLD-FASHIONED FUNGICIDE

Ordinary household baking soda is a natural fungicide. Mix up a solution of 1 tablespoon of baking soda in a gallon (4 l) of water, with a few drops of insecticidal soap or a couple of tablespoons of horticultural spray oil added to make it stick, and spray your plants with it weekly to prevent fungus diseases.

Fighting Disease

The most common problems in damp climates are fungal diseases. Mildews cause white patches on young leaves and distorted shoots and leaves with early leaf fall. Downy and powdery mildew occur on a whole range of plants from vines to roses to vegetables. Prevent it by keeping plants well spaced and ensuring good air circulation. Combat it by pruning out all infected stems and feeding the plants well. If a plant becomes badly infected, the only sure cure is to uproot it and seal it in a plastic bag in the trash. Don't be tempted to keep a badly infected plant in the garden; even if it recovers this time, it will always be prone to the disease and it is likely to infect others. Botrytis is another fungus that leaves a plant covered with mold. Again, prune out affected sections or prune the plant hard, and keep the soil in top condition.

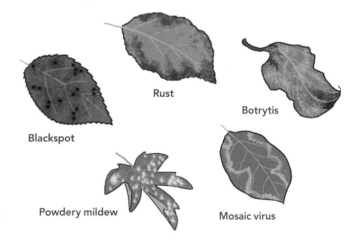

Rust

Botrytis

Blackspot

Powdery mildew

Mosaic virus

Mosaic virus can be a nuisance on many annual bedding plants and vegetables as well as some perennials. Leaves become yellow and distorted and are covered with small galls. The virus is spread by aphids and is generally incurable. Once plants are affected, get rid of them. Wash your hands thoroughly after you touch infected plants. To sterilize your tools, the usual solution of one part chlorine bleach to nine parts water won't work on mosaic virus. Disinfect your tools with a strong soap solution or by boiling them for five minutes instead.

All plants are susceptible to disease, and some are more at risk than others. Luckily there are relatively few diseases, and they vary from season to season. The important thing is to deal with the problem when you notice it and don't just hope it will go away on its own.

EXTENDING THE GROWING SEASON

Protecting your plants when the weather is cold can let you get an earlier start in the outdoor garden in spring, and keep plants going longer in fall.

THE SIMPLEST COLD FRAME

One old-timer's way to make a cold frame is to arrange four bales of straw to make the frame, and plant in the ground inside them. Cover the top with an old storm window from which you have removed the glass panes and putty and covered with a double layer of heavy-duty plastic.

The Cold Frame

A cold frame is simply a bottomless box with a removable clear or translucent top that lets in light. It provides a sheltered environment for plants to grow when the weather would otherwise be too cold for them. You can buy a ready-made cold frame, or make your own from a wood frame, stacked bricks, or concrete blocks and an old storm window. For maximum sun exposure the cold frame should face south, and the back needs to be slightly higher than the front so the lid sits on an angle. Some purchased cold frames have translucent sides that let in even more light.

Placing the cold frame with its back against a south-facing wall will provide maximum protection.

Your cold frame must have good ventilation so the temperature doesn't get too high and harm the plants inside and also to provide air circulation and let out excess moisture. Open the lid partway on sunny days.

Row Covers and Polytunnels

To protect plants in garden rows when they are first getting started in spring, or to prolong the harvest in fall, cover them with "floating" fabric row covers of lightweight spunbonded polyester. These covers allow light and moisture to penetrate and are light enough to be laid right over the plants without damaging them. Anchor the sides with U-shaped pins or stones to keep the fabric from blowing off.

To create a sort of mini-greenhouse in the garden, make tunnels by stretching plastic over a series of hoops. Make the tunnels high enough that they will not touch the tops of the plants. Be sure to use polyethylene, which will allow the plants to respire naturally. To allow for ventilation on sunny days, cut some slits in the plastic, or roll up the sides of the tunnel during the day.

COLD FRAME SOIL MIX

A good soil mix to use in a cold frame is 1 part topsoil or garden soil, 1 part composted manure, 1 part sharp (builder's) sand, and 2 parts crumbled compost.

Cloches and Hot Caps

To protect individual plants when a cold night is forecast, cover them with glass cloches or plastic or heavy waxed paper hot caps. Place the covers over the plants at the end of the day and remove them in the morning. These devices don't provide a lot of frost protection, and they overheat easily on sunny days. But in a small garden they can keep a few favorite plants producing a bit longer in fall than if they were left uncovered. You can make a hot cap by cutting the bottom from a clean, empty, gallon-size plastic milk jug. Just set the jug over the plant you want to protect.

GROWING IN CONTAINERS

With a few containers you can make a garden wherever you are, on a balcony, a fire escape, or in a concrete yard. Container gardening is versatile and adaptable, and if you move, you can take your garden with you.

There are as many styles of container gardening as any other type of garden. The type of pot says a lot about you. You don't have to stick with pots you can buy in garden centers; be inventive and make your own from recycled tins and wooden boxes, even trash cans and old tires can become happy homes for plants. All any container needs is a hole or two at the bottom for drainage. Just fill it with a suitable soil mix, and you have the beginning of a garden.

It is important to use a good potting mix with lots of compost. Because your plants will have to get all their nutrition from a small area, they won't get the benefit of a living soil. Container soil needs to be able to hold moisture and nutrients well since plants in containers need to be watered more often than those in the ground. The potting mix also needs to drain well rather than forming puddles, and it needs a good structure so it doesn't turn into a dense soggy mass when it's wet. Even if you can get hold of good garden soil, don't use it in containers, and avoid standard multipurpose potting mix; it doesn't hold nutrition longterm. Instead use a loam-based mix with plenty of compost, and mix in some vermiculite or perlite to lighten the load if you are putting containers on a roof garden or a balcony where weight is an issue. Self-watering containers are efficient and labor saving. You can buy all sorts, and you should also fill your containers with water-retaining granules to prevent water waste.

You can grow almost anything in a container. Vegetables are favorites; one large wooden box can give you a mixture of salads all summer if you keep resowing. A plastic trash can with a few holes pierced in it makes a perfect growing place for potatoes. And tomatoes look pretty in decorative ceramic pots. Choose plants that look interesting for the longest time—a Brussels sprout plant wouldn't look compelling, but a pot of ruby or rainbow chard is beautiful for months. It's the same with flowers—containers are perfect for high-impact summer annuals that bloom profusely, for slightly exotic lilies and agapanthus, and the sweetest scented pinks.

Containers come in an enormous variety of shapes, sizes, and colors, giving you the freedom to be creative with your garden. Containers with hard, squared edges often suit more formal arrangements; rounded corners provide a softer feel.

Layering bulbs in a container lets you plant different varieties in the same pot, just at different depths. You can choose bulbs that result in a timed spread of flowering or ones that flower together.

GREENHOUSE GROWING

A greenhouse allows you to extend your growing season, so you can start seeds earlier in spring and bring tender plants inside for winter. You'll be able to grow a much wider range of plants than outdoors, including tender and more exotic species as well as all those delicious Mediterranean vegetables.

Glass and aluminum flat-pack greenhouses are convenient and good. Or you can get greenhouses with cedar woodwork or have one custom built. Victorian-style greenhouses are popular in countries such as England and are made from timber and glass above a solid brick wall and base. People are increasingly moving toward polycarbonate glazing rather than glass because of its safety and increased insulation values.

Make sure your greenhouse has plenty of ventilation, and be sure to think about heat. Ideally you want the space to be at least frost free and possibly warm enough to support tender seedlings and plants. You could connect to an electricity supply, but if this isn't convenient you can install a solar heat sink to keep the space above freezing. This is a means of drawing warm air through the greenhouse at no cost, without complicated wiring. Watering is the other main question—whether or not to install an automatic watering system. It's a good idea to weigh the cost of this against the convenience.

It isn't always possible to put a greenhouse in the ideal place in a garden, most of us have constraints unless we're starting from scratch. As long as your greenhouse is placed with the longest length facing the sun, it's going to be hotter than one that has one end toward the sun. So if you can face the ridge running East–West, that's perfect.

KEEP IT CLEAN

Keep your greenhouse clean. Don't treat it as a glazed extension to the garden shed, where the lawn mower and barbecue hibernate between summers. Cleanliness inside your greenhouse will help keep the bugs down and help you grow healthy, strong plants.

Your greenhouse will need appropriate foundations for its size. This can be done using poured concrete or with paving slabs.

AS BIG AS YOU CAN AFFORD

Always buy the biggest greenhouse you can afford or accommodate. Whatever you get, it will not be big enough. That's the basic rule.

Making a Greenhouse Heatsink

A greenhouse heatsink is very easy to assemble, and it will make a huge difference to the health and longevity of your plants. Keeping them warm at night and cool during hot summer days, the heatsink requires virtually no maintenance once it's up and running—this is the most efficient and natural way to care for your greenhouse plants. The fan sucks air from the top of the greenhouse where the air is hottest and pumps it through the waste pipe into the base of the heatsink hole. During the day the warmed air then rises through the heatsink, warming the heatsink material and cooling the air, which passes through a vent (more waste pipe) and back into the greenhouse. At nighttime the cool air at the top of the greenhouse is pushed through the warmed heatsink heating up the air and cooling down the heatsink material. This warm air then passes through the vent into the greenhouse, where it helps to keep up the temperature.

You will need

- 1 x 10 watt PV solar panel
- 1 x 12 v battery
- 1 x small fan, such as one from an old computer
- 5-foot (1.5-m) length of 1.5-inch (38-mm) PVC waste pipe for heatsink pipe
- 1 x 3-foot (1-m) length of 1.5-inch (38-mm) PVC waste pipe for heatsink vent
- 3 cubic feet (1 m) of pea gravel or crushed glass
- Sheet insulation material

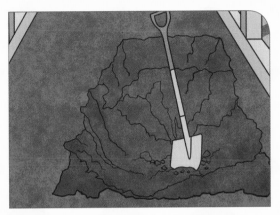

1 Dig a hole at least 3 feet (1 m) wide and deep in your greenhouse floor.

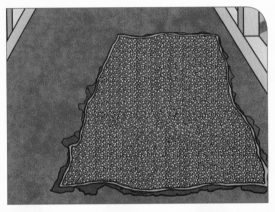

2 Line it with sheet insulation material and fill it with pea gravel or crushed glass.

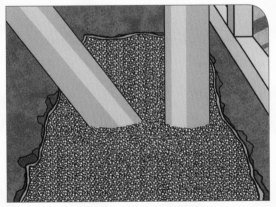

3 Insert the PVC wastepipe into the gravel vertically for the main pipe, and one at an angle for the vent.

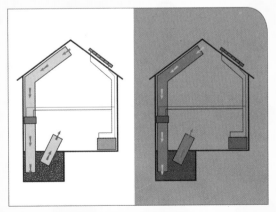

4 Attach the PVC pipe for the vent as illustrated above. Once in place attach a solar panel to the 12 v battery to drive the small fan 24 hours a day.

INDEX

Page reference in **boldface** indicates illustration

RESOURCES

Listed below are associations that can provide additional information as well as suppliers of seeds, equipment, and tools. All of these companies have websites. If you don't have a computer at home, you can visit a local library and seek the help of staff.

In the United States

Fedco Seeds
Provider of cold-hardy varieties and gardening supplies
P.O. Box 520
Waterville, ME 04903
(207) 873-7333
www.fedcoseeds.com

Johnny's Seeds
Provider of seeds and gardening supplies
955 Benton Avenue
Winslow, ME 04901
(877) 564-6697
www.johnnyseeds.com

National Gardening Association
Information on home, school, and community gardening
1100 Dorset Street
South Burlington, VT 05403
(802) 863-5251
www.garden.org

Seeds Savers Exchange
A nonprofit, member supported organization that saves and shares heirloom seeds
3094 North Winn Road
Decorah, Iowa 52101
(563) 382-5990
www.seedsavers.org

Cooperative State Research, Education, and Extension Service
A good place to start when embarking on any homesteading type activity
1400 Independence Avenue, Stop 2201
Washington, D.C. 20250-2201
(202) 720-4423
www.csrees.usda.gov/extension/

National Sustainable Agriculture Information Service
Latest news in sustainable agriculture and organic farming
P.O. Box 3657
Fayetteville, AR 72702
www.attra.org

U.S. Department of Agriculture
Publications on a wide range of topics, especially gardening and food preservation
1400 Independence Avenue
Washington, D.C. 20250
(202) 720-2791
www.usda.gov

In Canada

Lee Valley Tools Ltd.
Tools, books, and DVDs to help with fruit and vegetable gardening, seeding, pruning, and pest control. Extensive hardware catalog for custom racks, boxes, and shelving
P.O. Box 6295, Station J
Ottawa, Ont. K2A 1T4
(800) 267-8767 or (613) 596-0350
www.leevalley.com

Salt Spring Seeds
British Columbia-based producers and suppliers of untreated, non-GMO seeds for growing many types of produce
Box 444, Ganges P.O.
Salt Spring Island, B.C.
V8K 2W1
www.saltspringseeds.com